A TRANSLATORS HANDBOOK
ON PAUL'S LETTERS TO THE
COLOSSIANS
AND TO
PHILEMON

Helps for Translators

A HANDBOOK ON

Paul's Letters to the Colossians and to Philemon

by Robert G. Bratcher

and Eugene A. Nida

UBS Handbook Series

United Bible Societies
New York

The text of the Revised Standard Version used in this publication is copyrighted 1946, 1952, © 1971, 1973 by the Division of Christian Education of the National Council of the Churches of Christ in the U.S.A., and used by permission.

Quotations from Today's English Version are used by permission of the copyright owner, the American Bible Society, © 1966, 1971, 1976.

Printed in the United States of America

Books in the series of **Helps for Translators** may be ordered from a national Bible Society, or from either of the following centers:

United Bible Societies
European Production Fund
W-7000 Stuttgart 80
Postfach 81 03 40
Germany

United Bible Societies
1865 Broadway
New York, New York 10023
U.S.A.

L. C. Cataloging-in-Publication Data:

Bratcher, Robert G.
    [Translator's handbook on Paul's letters to the Colossians and to Philemon]
    A handbook on Paul's letters to the Colossians and to Philemon / by Robert G. Bratcher and Eugene A. Nida.
        p.   cm. — (UBS helps for translators) (UBS handbook series)
    Originally published under title: A translator's handbook on Paul's letters to the Colossians and to Philemon.
    Includes bibliographical references and index.
    ISBN 0-8267-0166-3 : $7.95
    1. Bible. N.T. Colossians—Translating. 2. Bible. N.T. Philemon—Translating. I. Nida, Eugene Albert. 1914- .
II. Title. III. Series. IV. Series: Helps for translators.
BS2715.5.B7   1993
227'.7077—dc20   92-20512
                                                              CIP

ABS-1993-200-2,500-CM-5-102692

P R E F A C E

A Translators Handbook on Paul's Letters to the Colossians and to Philemon follows the pattern already established in the more recent volumes in this series. Attention is paid to the structure of the discourse, as well as to words, phrases, and clauses, so as to allow the translator to understand as well as possible the movement and development of the letters as a whole, and not just the separate meaning of individual sentences.

Both the TEV and the RSV translations are cited at the beginning of each section under discussion; after that, for individual verses, the TEV alone is reproduced. In the discussion, the wording of the TEV text is underlined; the RSV text (as well as the text of other translations) is cited within quotation marks.

No attempt has been made to be exhaustive in the discussion of textual, exegetical, and translational matters; representative points of view are cited where important differences arise, and the translator is urged to consult the volumes cited in the Bibliography for further comments on such matters. There is a Glossary that explains certain technical terms, and an Index is provided that locates by page numbers some of the more important words and subjects dealt with in the Handbook.

Special thanks are due to Paul C. Clarke and Terry Jennings for their valuable help in the editing and preparation of the text for offset reproduction

> Robert G. Bratcher
> Eugene A. Nida

October 1977

CONTENTS

ABBREVIATIONS USED IN THIS VOLUME

Bible texts and versions cited (for details see Bibliography, page 137):

BJ	Bible de Jérusalem (French)
Brc	Barclay
BrCL	Brazilian common language translation
DuCL	Dutch common language translation
FrCL	French common language translation
Gdp	Goodspeed
GeCL	German common language translation
JB	Jerusalem Bible (English)
KJV	King James Version
Mft	Moffatt
NAB	New American Bible
NEB	New English Bible
NIV	New International Version
Phps	Phillips
RSV	Revised Standard Version
Seg	Segond
SpCL	Spanish common language translation
TC	Twentieth Century New Testament
TEV	Today's English Version
TNT	Translator's New Testament
TOB	Traduction Oecumenique de la Bible
Vg	Latin Vulgate
Wey	Weymouth

Books of the Bible:

Col	Colossians	Matt	Matthew
Cor	Corinthians	Phil	Philippians
Deut	Deuteronomy	Psa	Psalms
Eph	Ephesians	Rev	Revelation
Gal	Galatians	Rom	Romans
Gen	Genesis	Thes	Thessalonians
Heb	Hebrews		

Other abbreviations:

e.g.	*exempli gratia* = for example
ff.	= and the following (verses)
i.e.	id est = that is
LXX	Septuagint (see Glossary)
UBS	United Bible Societies
A&G	W.F. Arndt and F.W. Gingrich, A Greek-English Lexicon of the New Testament
Bl-D	F. Blass and A. Debrunner, A Greek Grammar of the New Testament

TRANSLATING COLOSSIANS

Paul wrote this letter to the church at Colossae while he was in prison
(4.3,18). Associated with him in the writing of the letter is Timothy
(1.1), and greetings are sent from six other individuals who are also
with Paul: Aristarchus, Mark, Joshua (also called Justus), Epaphras,
Luke, and Demas (4.10-14). The letter is to be taken to Colossae by
Tychicus, accompanied by Onesimus, who is from Colossae (4.7-9). A personal message is sent to Archippus (4.17).

There are obvious connections between Colossians and Philemon.
When Paul writes to Philemon, he is also in prison (Philemon 1.23), and
Timothy is associated with him in writing the letter (1). Of the six
individuals who appear in Colossians as sending greetings, five of them
appear also in Philemon (23-24). The whole letter to Philemon has to do
with the slave Onesimus, who is returning to his master Philemon (8-20).
And Archippus is associated with Philemon as one of the recipients of
the letter (2).

Colossians is also somehow related to Ephesians. Besides the obvious similarities between the contents of the two letters, Paul is also
in prison (6.20) and Tychicus is being sent with the letter, with the
similar commission of letting the readers know how Paul is getting along
(6.21-22).

The explanation of these relations is the most varied possible,
and a translator should consult some commentaries and at least read the
other two letters closely before concentrating on Colossians.

There is no way of determining where Paul was in prison, whether
in Ephesus, Caesarea, or Rome. There is a wide divergence of opinion on
this question, and since it is impossible to ascertain where Paul was,
it is equally impossible to state when Paul wrote the letter. It seems
quite probable, however (unless one disputes the Pauline authorship of
Colossians, as some do), that Colossians was written at the same time
and place as Philemon.

The letter is written to Christians living in Colossae, a city in
what was then the Roman province of Asia (of which Ephesus was the
capital). The city was in the Lycus Valley, some 175 kilometers east of
Ephesus; it was about 17 kilometers east of Laodicea and 20 kilometers
southeast of Hierapolis, both of which are associated with Colossae in
the letter (2.1, 4.13,15-16).

It appears that Paul had not himself been involved in establishing
or furthering the Christian work in Colossae (1.4, 2.1). The work there
had been established by Epaphras (1.7) who was from Colossae (4.12), and
who at the time of the writing of the letter was with Paul (4.12-13).
Epaphras was also involved in the Christian work in Laodicea and Hierapolis (4.13).

The purpose of the letter emerges quite clearly from its contents.
Some people were teaching doctrines in Colossae which were contrary to
the Christian message. This false teaching called itself a "philosophy"
(2.8), and had, as its core, the belief in "the ruling spirits of the
universe" (2.8,20; see also 1.16, 2.10,15), who were regarded as intermediary beings between God and mankind, sharing his authority and exer-
cising control over people's lives. So they were to be worshiped (2.18,
23); certain rules were to be kept with regard to food and drink (2.16a,

[1]

20-21); and certain religious festivals and holy days were to be observed (2.16b).

The Colossian Christians would be Gentiles, not Jews, and it is difficult to assess the significance of the inclusion of the Sabbath in the rules being imposed (2.16) or of the reference to circumcision (2.11). It is significant that there are no OT quotations or allusions in the letter, and that the exposition about the person and work of Christ is made independently of any Jewish expectations about the Messiah. It seems quite clear--though this is impossible to prove--that Paul used some of the language of the false teachers in his exposition of the Christian message.

It appears that this false teaching was meant not to supplant the Christian faith but to supplement it. But Paul vigorously denies its validity and declares that to follow it is to abandon Christ (2.8). His readers are called to be loyal to the true message about Christ, and what he has done for all who believe in him.

The letter opens with the standard Pauline salutation, and the body of the letter falls naturally into two parts: exposition and ex-hortation. Some final admonitions follow, after which come personal messages, greetings, and the closing benediction.

Outline of Contents

A. Salutation (1.1-2)

B. Expository Section (1.3--2.23)

    1. Prayer of Thanksgiving (1.3-8)
    2. Prayer of Petition (1.9-14)
    3. The Person and Work of Christ (1.15-20)
    4. Exhortation (1.21-23)
    5. Paul's Apostolic Ministry and Message (1.24--2.5)
    6. The New Life in Christ (2.6-15)
    7. Freedom from Legalism (2.16-23)

C. Hortatory Section (3.1--4.1)

    1. Exhortation to Live the New Life (3.1-4)
    2. Christian Character and Conduct (3.5-17)
    3. The Christian Household (3.18--4.1)

D. Final Admonitions (4.2-6)

E. Closing Messages and Greetings (4.7-18)

Today's English Version   (1.1-2)   Revised Standard Version

1 From Paul, who by God's will   1 Paul, an apostle of Christ
is an apostle of Christ Jesus,   Jesus by the will of God, and
and from our brother Timothy--   Timothy our brother,
2 To God's people in Colossae,   2 To the saints and faithful
who are our faithful brothers in   brethren in Christ at Colossae:
union with Christ;   Grace to you and peace from
May God our Father give you   God our Father.
grace and peace.

The letter begins with the usual salutation, common to nearly all of Paul's letters: (1) an identification of the writer, or writers of the letter; (2) the recipients; and (3) a Christian salutation.

Newman has taken up the problem of the salutations in the letters of the NT, and shows how they can be restructured in terms of contemporary Western custom in writing of letters. For Colossians he proposes [using Today's English Version (TEV) language] that the letter begin:

1.2   To God's people in Colossae, who are our faithful
           brothers in union with Christ:
           May God our Father give you grace and peace.

The ending would place 1.1 after 4.18, in the following order:

4.18; 1.1   May God's grace be with you. Do not forget my chains!
             With my own hand I sign this letter: Greetings from
             Paul, who by God's will is an apostle of Christ Jesus,
             and from our brother Timothy.[1]

Each translator will consider the possible advantages and disadvantages of such restructuring, in terms of his readers.

1.1   From Paul, who by God's will is an apostle of Christ
             Jesus, and from our brother Timothy--

In some languages it may be quite impossible to begin a document with the phrase "from Paul," especially when Paul is himself the writer of the letter, that is to say, it may not be possible for an author to speak of himself in the third person. The identification of the writer may require a first person singular pronoun followed by a verb indicating "writing," for example, "I Paul write to..."

Paul's status as an apostle of Christ Jesus is the result of God's doing; it was God who made Paul an apostle (2 Cor 1.1, Eph 1.1, and 2 Tim 1.1 have the identical phrase; Rom 1.1 has "a called apostle," and 1 Cor 1.1 "a called apostle of Christ Jesus through the will of God"). Apostle is literally "messenger" and has the meaning of a representative, with the commission and authority to act in the name and on behalf of the

[3]

one who has sent him; he is not simply one who delivers a message and nothing else.

The phrase by God's will may be rendered in some languages as "this is what God wanted" or "this is what God planned." In other instances, it may be better to restructure God's will as a causative, for example, "God caused me to be an apostle of Christ Jesus."

The relationship between apostle and Christ Jesus must be expressed in some languages as "an apostle sent by Christ Jesus" or "an apostle especially commissioned by Christ Jesus." Though the term apostle may be rendered by a word meaning simply "messenger," it is important to avoid the connotation of "errand boy." The importance of the message communicated by the apostle, as well as the special relationship between the apostle and the one who sent him, must be appropriately reflected. Sometimes this can be done by a phrase, "one who is sent with a special message."

Since the role of our brother Timothy is secondary in the writing of this letter, it may be useful to indicate this fact by some such phrase as "our brother Timothy joins me in greeting you" or "...in sending this letter to you."

It may be essential to avoid a word such as brother, since this might refer only to individuals of the same family. An appropriate equivalent is sometimes "our fellow Christian Timothy" or "Timothy who is also a Christian together with us." The rendering of our would of course be an inclusive first person plural if a distinction is made between so-called inclusive and exclusive first person plurals.

1.2   To God's people in Colossae, who are our faithful
         brothers in union with Christ;
         May God our Father give you grace and peace.

The form of the Greek text seems to require treating "saints" [Revised Standard Version (RSV)] as an adjective, modifying brothers, just as faithful does, since there is the one article with the whole phrase: "to our holy and faithful brothers." This is done by Barclay (Brc) "dedicated and loyal," New International Version (NIV) "holy and faithful," Moffatt (Mft) "consecrated and faithful," and Goodspeed (Gpd) "devoted and steadfast." But commentators (such as Lightfoot, Abbott, and Moule) take the word as a substantive, standing alone, as do the vast majority of translations.

God's people represents the Greek word which is used throughout the NT as a designation of Christians, in terms of the concept of the chosen people (Israel, in the OT) as those who belong exclusively to God, by his sovereign choice and determination; in these contexts the word does not have the idea of "holy" or "saintly," referring to moral and spiritual qualities.

Because of the need of modifying the way in which the writer is introduced in verse 1, it may be important to redistribute the contents of these first two verses, for example, "I Paul am writing to you who are God's people in Colossae," followed by an identification of Paul's role as an apostle, the relationship of Timothy to the letter, and finally some statement with regard to God's people in Colossae, for example, "It is God who has made me an apostle of Christ Jesus, and our brother Timothy joins me in this letter to you, who are our faithful fellow Christians in union with Christ." This introductory statement can then be followed by the actual salutation.

In some languages, it may be necessary to use a rather special form of possession in translating God's people. A literal rendering might suggest "God's slaves." It is important, therefore, to employ an expression which will indicate that these are "people dedicated to God" or "people who are God's followers."

The phrase in Colossae may require some expansion, for example, "people who live in Colossae" or "people whose homes are in the town of Colossae."

As in verse 1, it may also be necessary to translate brothers as "fellow Christians" or "fellow believers."

Some languages may require a goal for the adjective faithful, that is to say, it may be necessary to indicate to whom one is faithful. In this context, it would seem quite clear that God should be the one to whom these brothers are faithful, though one might argue that the term could imply loyalty to the Gospel or even loyalty to other believers.

In union with Christ represents the formula frequently used by Paul to describe the intimate relationship which exists between Christians and their Lord; this is a corporate reality, a relationship that exists between people who have a common loyalty and devotion to Jesus Christ as Savior and Lord. NEB translates this as "incorporate in Christ," while Brc renders it as "Christian fellowship." The German common language translation (GeCL) joins "in Christ" to "faithful," as follows: "who have faith in Christ," but this is not probable (see Moule).

The phrase in union with Christ is probably one of the most difficult expressions in the entire NT to render satisfactorily. In some instances, one can only use a clause "who are linked with Christ" or "who become, as it were, one with Christ." Only very rarely can one use a literal translation such as "in Christ."

The actual salutation is standard in all of Paul's letters; only in Romans (which adds "and from our Lord Jesus Christ") and 2 Thessalonians (which has simply "grace and peace to you") are the salutations different. Some important manuscripts add here "and from the Lord Jesus Christ"; see the Textual Commentary on the Greek New Testament for the reasons for rejecting that addition here.

Grace is the one word which most vividly expresses God's unconditional, unmerited, uncaused love and favor which he displays toward mankind in Christ. In the stereotyped formula of a salutation, however, it most probably refers to the result of God's attitude in terms of blessing, so that its verbal equivalent would be, "May God bless you" or "be kind to you." Peace is a word with its roots in the OT concept of salvation as wholeness, completeness, the full and abundant life enjoyed by God's people because of their relationship to one another and to God. It is the new quality of life enjoyed by those who are in the fellowship of the people of God. As part of the salutation, its main emphasis is probably the lack of conflict and dissension in the Christian fellowship.

Sometimes the only way in which one may introduce the strong desire expressed in the salutation May God our Father give you grace and peace is to introduce this by some expression for prayer or supplication, for example, "I pray that God our Father may give you grace and peace" or "I ask God our Father to give you grace and peace."

In some instances, one cannot use the appositional expression God our Father but must employ a clause as an attributive to "God," for example, "God who is our father."

Give you grace may be expressed as "show you his love" or "cause good to come to you."

Peace may often be best expressed metaphorically, for example, "may God cause you to have a quiet heart" or "...to sit down in your hearts." This emphasis of peace in this type of context is not, however, mere tranquility or so-called "peace of mind." It is far more all-embracing and therefore should suggest what is often spoken of in English as "the good life."

TEV	(1.3-8)	RSV

PRAYER OF THANKSGIVING

3 We always give thanks to God, the Father of our Lord Jesus Christ, when we pray for you. 4 For we have heard of your faith in Christ Jesus and of your love for all God's people. 5 When the true message, the Good News, first came to you, you heard about the hope it offers. So your faith and love are based on what you hope for, which is kept safe for you in heaven. 6 The gospel keeps bringing blessings and is spreading throughout the world, just as it has among you ever since the day you first heard about the grace of God and came to know it as it really is. 7 You learned of God's grace from Epaphras, our dear fellow servant, who is Christ's faithful worker on our[a] behalf. 8 He has told us of the love that the Spirit has given you.

[a]our; some manuscripts have your.

3 We always thank God, the Father of our Lord Jesus Christ, when we pray for you, 4 because we have heard of your faith in Christ Jesus and of the love which you have for all the saints, 5 because of the hope laid up for you in heaven. Of this you have heard before in the word of the truth, the gospel 6 which has come to you, as indeed in the whole world it is bearing fruit and growing--so among yourselves, from the day you heard and understood the grace of God in truth, 7 as you learned it from Epaphras our beloved fellow servant. He is a faithful minister of Christ on our[a] behalf 8 and has made known to us your love in the Spirit.

[a]other ancient authorities read your

This whole section is one sentence in Greek, with a minor break at the end of verse 6. It is a prayer of thanksgiving, the usual pattern Paul follows in his letters, except Galatians. Certain key words occur: faith (4), love (4,8), hope (5), gospel (5), truth (5,6), grace (6). The prayer proceeds backward, from the faith and love of the Colossians (verse 4), which is based on the hope reserved for them in heaven, of which they heard when the gospel was announced to them (verses 5-6) by Epaphras (verse 7), who had told Paul of their love (verse 8). This sentence may be restructured partially or completely, to follow a more or less chronological or logical order, for example, Epaphras told us about you, how you received the message (verses 7-8), what it did for you (verses 5-6), and how it resulted in your faith and love (verse 4). But the advantages of such restructuring should clearly outweigh its disadvantages. Newman proposes the following restructuring of verses 6-8: [6-7]The gospel keeps spreading and reaching more people throughout the world, just as it has among you ever since the day you first heard of the grace of God from Epaphras, our dear fellow servant who is Christ's faithful worker on our behalf. Through him you learned of God's grace and came to know what it is all about, [8]and he has told us of the love that the Spirit has given you.

Some translations combine the two sections 3-8 and 9-14 into one, for example, GeCL "Thanksgiving and Petition," Jerusalem Bible (JB) and NIV "Thanksgiving and Prayer."

1.3   We always give thanks to God, the Father of our
           Lord Jesus Christ, when we pray for you.

We: the question is whether or not this plural is genuine. Is it an "epistolary" plural, that is, a conventional way of referring to the writer himself, without consciously including others, or is it a real plural? Some (for example, GeCL) take it as singular. In the light of (1) the singulars that occur (1.23, 24-27,29; 2.1-5; 4.3b-4; 4.7-9,10,18), and (2) the deliberate switch from the plural to singular (1.28,29; 4.3a,3b), it seems probable that the plurals are real (1.3-8, 9-14,28; 4.3a,8b), and Paul intends to associate with himself not only Timothy (who is named in 1.1), but also the others of his immediate group. (The inclusive first person plurals, as in 1.13-14, fall into another category.)

Always is taken by most commentators and translations to modify we give thanks; some, however [see Traduction Oecuménique de la Bible (TOB)], take it to modify we pray.

In a number of languages, it is almost obligatory to indicate the reason for thanks being given. This means that in the first clause of verse 3, it may be important to say "we always give thanks to God because of you" or "...because of who you are."

Since the expression of thanks implies words, it must be expressed in some languages as direct discourse, for example, "we always say to God, We thank you."

To God, the Father of our Lord Jesus Christ: some important manuscripts have "to the God and Father of our Lord Jesus Christ" (as in Rom 15.6, 1 Cor 15.24, 2 Cor 1.3, Eph 3.1, etc.), but very few [for example, King James Version (KJV) Mft] follow such a reading.

[7]

Though the relationship of the Lord Jesus Christ to the Father is biologically different from what exists in purely human relations, this is a figurative expression which occurs so frequently in the Scriptures and is so important in the entire structure of Christian thought that it needs to be preserved in a more or less literal form. The apposition God, the Father of our Lord Jesus Christ must, of course, be expressed in some languages as a type of attributive by a relative clause, for example, "God who is the father of our Lord Jesus Christ."

In a number of lanugages, one cannot speak of "our Lord," for individuals do not, in a sense, possess their Lord; rather, they obey him or are his followers. In some instances, our Lord must be rendered as "the chief over us," or even "the one who commands us," or "the Lord to whom we are obedient."

The name Jesus Christ should be taken as more or less equivalent to a proper name. It is perfectly possible in a footnote to indicate the meaning of Jesus as it is related to the OT name of Joshua, but the significance of the name can best be indicated by referring to Matt 1.21. Some translators have always wanted to translate Christ as "the Messiah," or "the annointed one," or "the one specially designated by God," but all of these designations become unusually heavy, and though useful as background information, are not recommended for inclusion within a text.

The clause when we pray for you refers not merely to a particular event but a whole succession of events and therefore is better rendered in a number of languages as "whenever we pray for you."

In a number of languages, it is important with a verb "to pray" to indicate clearly to whom prayer is directed, and therefore it may be necessary to say "whenever we pray to God for you," or "whenever we mention you in our prayers to God."

Since prayer inevitably suggests some kind of verbal form, it may be necessary to render this as direct discourse, for example, "whenever we say to God, May you be good to the Christians in Colossae."

1.4   For we have heard of your faith in Christ Jesus
         and of your love for all God's people.

For we have heard: in Greek this is an aorist participle, subordinate to the main verb we give thanks, either temporal in force ("after having heard") or, which is more likely, causative, as in TEV. The news about this came from Epaphras (verse 8).

Since we have heard of your faith is related to giving thanks to God rather than to we pray for you, it may be important to repeat the first part of verse 3 at the beginning of verse 4, for example, "we give thanks to God because we have heard of your faith"; otherwise, the meaning might be interpreted in the sense that "we pray for you because we have heard of your faith."

Your faith in: the use here of the preposition en (and not eis) has led some (for example, Lightfoot, Moule; Turner less certainly) to hold that Christ Jesus represents the sphere in which the faith is exercised, not the object of faith; thus NEB "the faith you hold in Christ Jesus," and GeCL "your faith which unites you with Jesus Christ." Most translators, however, have not been convinced, and, like TEV and RSV, translate simply faith in, making Christ Jesus the object of faith.

Since faith in this context is a matter of active trust and confidence, it may be appropriate to translate your faith in Christ Jesus as "how you trust Christ Jesus" or "how you have put your confidence in Christ Jesus." Similarly, of your love for all God's people may be rendered as "how you love all God's people."

For God's people see verse 2.

1.5   When the true message, the Good News, first came
       to you, you heard about the hope it offers. So
       your faith and love are based on what you hope for,
       which is kept safe for you in heaven.

In Greek (see RSV) the sentence continues without interruption; TEV has quite radically reconstructed the verse; see also Phillips (Phps) Translator's New Testament (TNT) Brc NEB.

The true message, the Good News: in Greek this phrase is preceded by the preposition en, which some take instrumentally, that is, the gospel was the means by which they heard; it could be taken temporally, "in the time when" (so Moule; Turner admits this is possible). What Paul clearly intends to say is that the Colossians heard of this hope the first time the gospel was announced to them. The gospel is described as the word of truth. The word (ho logos) may be the act of preaching, proclamation, so that "the truth (of) the gospel" can be taken to mean "the true gospel," as contrasted with the false message proclaimed by the heretics (so Lightfoot Moule NEB TNT); or else, "the true message of the gospel" [Gpd Twentieth Century (TC)]; or else, "the gospel" is taken in apposition, "the true message, that is, the gospel" [so TEV GeCL New American Bible (NAB); compare Abbott].

In some languages, the concept of true is expressed in one of two different ways. One may speak of (1) "a message about what really happened" or (2) "a message which is worthy of being believed" or "a message which merits confidence." It is probably the latter of these forms of expressions which is more appropriate, especially in this type of context.

In a number of langugages, it is not possible to translate literally Good News since this would imply that in some way or other "news" has some moral quality of "goodness." A more satisfactory equivalent in a number of languages is "refreshing news," or "happy news," or "news which makes one happy."

The term News is frequently expressed as "recent words" or by some term which combines at least three different components, namely, "recent," "important," and "words."

First came to you, you heard: the compound verb "to hear before" occurs only here in the NT. Some take this "before" to refer to the time before the Colossians had actually hoped or to the time before receiving this letter; both of these possibilities seem highly unlikely. It seems more probable that it here refers to the "the first time" they heard the gospel [so NEB Gpd Phps French common language translation (FrCL); Mft "you heard of this hope originally"]. It was Epaphras who proclaimed the gospel to them (verse 7).

Frequently, one cannot speak of "Good News coming"; only animate objects may actually "come," and therefore, in this context it may be useful to use some such expression as "when you were first told about the good news" or "when for the first time someone announced the good news to you."

It is quite clear that the hope does not here represent the attitude of hoping, held by the Colossians, since it is impossible to say that one's attitude of hoping can be kept safe in heaven, that is, with God; it is, rather, the object of the Colossians' hope that is kept safe in heaven. This object (as of faith) is, finally, Christ or God himself; but in this context, it seems not to be personal, but to refer to the reward that is kept safe in heaven for God's people. In general, in the NT "hope" is not simply an uncertain expectation or an unfounded desire; it is assurance, confidence, certainty.

Since the hope refers to the object for which one hopes, it may be important to express the hope by a clause, for example, "you heard about what you can hope for." The term hope involves several important and closely related components of meaning. There is an element of time, often expressed as "waiting for." A second element suggests some measure of patience, and a third factor is something good which is to happen at the end of a period of waiting. Thus, in this sense, hope is the opposite of "dread." It may, therefore, be appropriate, in this context, to translate you heard about the hope it offers as "you heard about what the good news says concerning that good which you may expect, as you wait in confidence for it."

There may be problems involved in speaking of "the Good News offering hope," but one can usually speak of "the good news which talks about hope," or "...which is a message about hope," or "...about what one may hope for."

In Greek, "the hope" is preceded by the preposition dia "because" (so RSV). Some take it here to mean that "the hope" is the foundation or source of the readers' faith and love. A connection is clearly intended, as TEV so and RSV "because" make explicit; see also GeCL ja auch.

The statement so your faith and love are based on what you hope for becomes especially complex in languages in which one cannot readily speak of faith and love as nouns but must render these as verbs. This inevitably results in considerable expansion, for example, "this means that the fact that you have confidence in Christ Jesus and love for God's people is the result of what you have hoped for" or, inversely, "what you hope for is what causes you to put confidence in Christ Jesus and love God's people."

The verb translated kept safe occurs only in three other passages in the NT: Luke 19.20, 2 Tim 4.8, and Heb 9.27 (where it is used impersonally). A similar passage (using different words) is found in 1 Peter 1.4. The verb means "put away for safekeeping," "store up," "keep safe."

A more or less literal rendering of kept safe almost immediately suggests that the object of one's hope is some physical object rather than the experience of the glory which will be the believer's in the future. Futhermore, in some languages, it is important to render the passive is kept safe as an active verb with the agent, namely, God. There-

fore, one must say "God is keeping safe for you in heaven what you are
hoping for" or "...for you in heaven the reward that you are confident
God will give to you."

In a number of languages, an important distinction is made between
"heaven" as the sky and "heaven" as the abode of God. This latter meaning
must then be expressed as "where God is" or "where God dwells."

1.6   The gospel keeps bringing blessings and is
                spreading throughout the world, just as it has
                among you ever since the day you first heard
                about the grace of God and came to know it as
                it really is.

Because of restructuring, "which has come to you" (RSV) appears in
TEV in verse 5, came to you, and in the beginning of verse 6, the subject
is introduced again, the gospel. What follows is the statement of the
effectiveness and growth of the gospel throughout the world, as among the
Colossians. The idea of the gospel "bearing fruit" (RSV) is a bit odd,
unless it is taken as the power of the gospel to produce results and to
continue to increase its effects among people everywhere. For other uses
of the verb karpophoreō "to bear fruit" in a metaphorical sense, see Mark
4.20; Luke 8.15; Col 1.10. Here only does the verb occur in the middle
voice (not active, as elsewhere). Lightfoot calls it a "dynamic" middle,
the Gospel as it inherently is. "The middle is intensive, the active
extensive." The two verbs, say Lightfoot, denote the inner working and
the outward extension of the gospel.[5]

It may be quite impossible, in some instances, to speak of "the
gospel bringing blessings." This could only be done by a person rather
than a message. Therefore, it may be important to render the gospel keeps
bringing blessings as the "the good news continually causes blessings for
people," or "causes good to happen to people," or "...causes good for
people."

It is frequently quite impossible to say "the gospel...is spreading
throughout the world," for the gospel, in a sense, is not a mass like
water or sand, but like a living vine which spreads and bears fruit. It
is a message which must be heard, and therefore, the equivalent expression
may be "more and more people in the world are hearing the good news,"
or "the good news is being spoken to more and more people," or "...is
being announced to people everywhere in the world."

Paul's reference to throughout the world is, of course, to be understood in terms of the Graeco-Roman world, for this was the civilized
world in New Testament times. In translation, however, it does not seem
to be important or necessary to make any special distinction, though
one might wish to introduce a footnote to explain the evident intent of
this expression.

Just as it has among you should be related not only to the spreading
of the good news but also the fact that it brings blessings. This may be
rendered in some cases as "just as it has been doing all this among you."

Ever since the day you first heard may be rendered as "beginning with the day when you first heard" or "from the first day that you heard even until now."

The grace of God represents all that God is in his attitude of love, goodness, and forgiveness toward mankind. In this type of context, the grace of God may perhaps be most effectively rendered as "God's goodness to people" or "God's kindness to people." Some translators wish to introduce the concept of "unmerited goodness," that is to say, "goodness to people when they did not deserve it," but this often results in a rather heavy expression which may appear more negative rather than positive, for it is God's "loving goodness" which needs to be emphasized.

To know is in Greek a compound verb, which may carry the connotation of knowing thoroughly, completely. The use of know in this context suggests something more than mere intellectual perception or "knowing about." The implication is "having some experience of." This is in line with such biblical expressions as "knowing God," which certainly involves more than mere intellectual knowledge about God.

As it really is is what is meant by "in truth." The final expression in verse 6 came to know it as it really is may be difficult to express clearly and in a few words. The idea is essentially "and experienced just how God is loving and good to you" or "really experienced what it means to have God be so kind to you."

1.7   You learned of God's grace from Epaphras, our dear fellow servant, who is Christ's faithful worker on our[a] behalf.

[a]our; some manuscripts have your.

It is important to avoid rendering learned with a term which would suggest a person being a student of something. It may, therefore, be more satisfactory to restructure the first clause you learned of God's grace from Epaphras to read "Epaphras was the one who told you about God's grace."

Epaphras...fellow servant...faithful worker: in Greek the first noun is sundoulos, commonly rendered "fellow slave," and the second one is diakonos, usually rendered "servant." Since today the word "slave" carries overtones which may not make it acceptable, "servant" is used and diakonos is rendered "worker" (so Brc). RSV Phps NIV use "servant" and "minister."

A literal rendering of our dear fellow servant might suggest that Epaphras was a servant of Paul. It may, therefore, be necessary to translate our dear fellow servant as "one who serves Christ along with us and who is dear to us" or "...one whom we love."

On our behalf: United Bible Societies Greek New Testament (UBS Gk NT) has changed from "our" (hēmōn) in the 2nd edition to "your" (humōn) in the 3rd edition. Textual evidence in favor of "our" certainly seems stronger than for "your," but other considerations (see Textual Commentary) have a bearing on the matter. Preferring "our" are: Lightfoot, Abbott, Pcake, Moule: NEB RSV JB NAB NIV TNT Brc Gpd FrCL TOB; in favor of "your" are Vg Phps Mft GeCL Spanish common language translation (SpCL).

On our behalf means that Epaphras was doing the work among the Colossians that Paul and his companions wanted to do but could not.

The expression Christ's...worker may be expressed in many languages as "one who works for Christ" or "one who helps Christ." The term faithful is not to be understood in the sense of "full of faith" but as "loyal to Christ" or as "one who can be trusted."

On our behalf can be rendered as "this is a help to us" or "in this way Epaphras helps us." If, however, the textual alternative "your" is to be understood, then one may say "this is a help to you" or "in this way Epaphras helps you."

1.8   He has told us of the love that the Spirit has
           given you.

Told represents a verb used infrequently in the NT (7 times), and has the sense of "make plain, clear."

The love that the Spirit has given you represents the literal "your love in (the) spirit." There is much uncertainty about the meaning of this phrase. Commentators point out that Paul does not refer to the Holy Spirit in Colossians, unless this phrase is such a reference (see also TEV in 1.9; the other occurrence of pneuma is 2.5, where it refers to Paul's own spirit). As Moule says, it may be simply "your more than merely human love." NEB has "your God-given love," Phps "Christian love," TNT "the love which the Spirit has inspired in you" (similarly Brc), Gpd "love which the Spirit has awakened in you" (TOB similarly); GeCL is more explicit, "...God's Spirit..."; Dutch common language translation (DuCL) has "your love whose source is the Spirit."

Love here may be the love for all fellow Christians (as in verse 4), or it could be the Colossians' love for Paul and his companions.

It is rare that one can speak of "love" without designating the object of love. The relationship of the Spirit to this love is probably best understood as causative, and therefore, if love must be expressed as a verb, perhaps one can render verse 8 as "he has told us how the Spirit has caused you to love fellow Christians" or "...love us."

TEV	(1.9-14)	RSV

9 For this reason we have always prayed for you, ever since we heard about you. We ask God to fill you with the knowledge of his will, with all the wisdom and understanding that his Spirit gives. 10 Then you will be able to live as the Lord wants and will always do what pleases him. Your lives will produce all kinds of good deeds, and you will grow in your knowledge of God. 11-12 May you be made strong with all

9 And so, from the day we heard of it, we have not ceased to pray for you, asking that you may be filled with the knowledge of his will in all spiritual wisdom and understanding, 10 to lead a life worthy of the Lord, fully pleasing to him, bearing fruit in every good work and increasing in the knowledge of God. 11 May you be strengthened with all power, according to his glorious might, for all endurance and patience with joy, 12 giving thanks to the Father, who has

the strength which comes from his glorious power, so that you may be able to endure everything with patience. And with joy give thanks to[b] the Father, who has made you fit to have your share of what God has reserved for his people in the kingdom of light. 13 He rescued us from the power of darkness and brought us safe into the kingdom of his dear Son, 14 by whom we are set free, that is, our sins are forgiven.

[b]with patience. And with joy give thanks to; or with patience and joy. And give thanks to.

qualified us[b] to share in the inheritance of the saints in light. 13 He has delivered us from the dominion of darkness and transferred us to the kingdom of his beloved Son, 14 in whom we have redemption, the forgiveness of sins.

[b]Other ancient authorities read you

Following the prayer of thanksgiving for the Colossians' spiritual progress, Paul continues, "for this reason we have always prayed for you," and, without a break (verses 9-12), lists the virtues he and his companions pray that God will give the Colossians, ending with the petition that they will give thanks to God (verse 12), who has enabled them to receive his gifts. The structure of verses 9-12 is as follows: the main verb is "we do not cease praying and asking" followed by the content of the petition, "that you be filled," whose purpose or result (verse 10), is expressed by the infinitive "to live," which is modified by a succession of circumstantial participles, "bearing fruit and growing" (verse 10), "being made strong" (verse 11), and "giving thanks" (verse 12). The mention of "light" (verse 12) leads Paul to expand on God's redemptive activity through his Son (verses 13-14). These last two verses do not fit into the category of "prayer of petition" but are theological reflection which serves as a transition to the following section, a hymn about the person and work of Christ. Some scholars place verses 13-14 with the next section, but it seems preferable to keep them with this section; verses 15-20 show signs of being a unit. The question of the first person plural (verse 9) should be handled in the same way as in the previous section (see verse 3).

1.9   For this reason we have always prayed for you, ever since we heard about you. We ask God to fill you with the knowledge of his will, with all the wisdom and understanding that his Spirit gives.

The phrase for this reason should not refer specifically to the love which the believers in Colossae had manifested, but to all of their experience in Christian faith. It may, therefore, be necessary in some cases to use a transitional expression which will be more inclusive, for example, "because of all this," or "because of all you have experienced," or "because of all that has happened to you."

We have always prayed represents the Greek "we never stop praying," which is not to be taken literally, of course. In the place of we have always prayed, one may more appropriately translate this in some instances as "we continued to pray."

Ever since we heard about you may be rendered as "beginning the first day we heard about you and even until now" or "we began praying for you when we first heard about you and we still do."

We ask God to fill you represents the passive "asking that you be filled"; the active is used in order to make God explicit, as the one who does the filling. Other ways may be sought to express the idea of "fill": compare TNT "you may be completely certain"; Brc "have complete insight"; NEB "you may receive from him...for full insight."

To fill you with the knowledge is essentially a causative expression and, therefore, may be best rendered in some languages as "to cause you to have knowledge" or "to cause you to experience." In those instances, in which languages require direct discourse, one may say, "We ask God, Cause the believers in Colossae to know..."

Knowledge is here the compound noun, related to the verb "to know" in verse 7. As commentators point out, this is not merely intellectual perception, but living relationship.

His will is, in this context, God's design, purpose, plan, intention for his people. The knowledge of his will is really "to experience what God wants for you." This may be expressed as "to experience what God wants you to do," but more likely as "to experience what God wants you to experience."

Wisdom and understanding: the word "wisdom" (sophia) is used often in the NT, and in Colossians it appears further in 1.28; 2.3,23; 3.16; 4.5; "understanding" (sunesis) appears once more in Colossians (2.2), and in 5 other places in the NT: Mark 12.33, Luke 2.47, 1 Cor 1.19 (from Isa 29.14), Eph 3.4, 2 Tim 2.7. No sharp difference in meaning is to be sought between the two words: they are joined together for emphasis to denote complete apprehension, knowledge, of God's will.

The relation of "all spiritual wisdom and understanding" (RSV) to the preceding the knowledge of his will, as expressed by the preposition "in" (RSV), is perhaps one of means; it is by means of all spiritual wisdom and understanding that the Colossians will have the knowledge of God's will. Since wisdom and understanding are essentially the means by which the believers in Colossae would experience God's will, this relationship may be expressed as a causative, "being wise and having understanding will cause you to know God's will."

That his Spirit gives translates the Greek adjective "spiritual." Many translate "all spiritual wisdom and understanding," which may better represent the intention of the text. Only GeCL and FrCL do as TEV has done, making it an explicit reference to God's Spirit as the source of wisdom and understanding (so Abbott, Peake). Or it can also be taken to mean "wisdom and understanding about spiritual matters." But it may be said that with Paul such "spiritual" knowledge is ultimately from (the Spirit of) God. Since the relationship of the Spirit of God to wisdom and understanding is perhaps best interpreted as causative, one may say "which God's Spirit causes you to have." This causative relationship may, therefore, be combined with the previous as "God's Spirit causes you to be wise and have understanding and this causes you to know God's will."

1.10   Then you will be able to live as the Lord wants and
                 will always do what pleases him. Your lives will pro-
                 duce all kinds of good deeds, and you will grow in
                 your knowledge of God.

Then you will be able to live represents the infinitive of the verb "to walk," expressing the result or purpose of being filled with the knowledge of God's will. The Greek verb is often used in the metaphorical sense of manner of life (as the Heb hālak). Paul always uses it in a figurative sense: Col 2.6, 3.7, 4.5, 1 Thes 2.12, 4.1.

The transitional adverb then is not so much temporal as conditional, for example, "if then that is so" or "that being so."

Able to live is not a reference to a standard of living but to a manner of life or behavior. This may be expressed in some cases as "able to conduct yourself," or "able to do," or "able to carry on."

As the Lord wants is an adverbial phrase "worthily of the Lord," that is, in a manner that is required by their status as the Lord's people (see "to walk...worthily of God" in 1 Thes 2.12). JB has "the kind of life which the Lord expects of you"; Phps "your lives...may bring credit to your master's name"; SpCL "that you conduct yourselves as people should who belong to the Lord"; GeCl "so to live as to bring honor to the Lord."

Always do what pleases him: the noun areskeia occurs only here in the NT; the verb areskō, with God or the Lord as object, is found in Rom 8.8, 1 Cor 7.32, 1 Thes 2.15 (not pleasing God), and 1 Thes 4.1, which offers the closest parallel: "to walk and to please God." "To please a person" may be expressed in some languages as "to cause a person to be happy." On the basis of such an expression, one may translate the latter part of the first sentence of verse 10 as "will always do what causes God to be happy."

All kinds of good deeds is joined to produce in TEV and others (so RSV "bearing fruit in every good work"), but it may be connected with the preceding to live. The literary figure known as chiasmus (a-b-b-a) is here employed: "in every good deed bearing fruit, and growing in the knowledge of God." The first line is attributive and verb, the second line verb and attributive.

It may not be possible to say "your lives will produce all kinds of good deeds." It is not literally the life which produces such deeds but the individual himself. Therefore, one may say "because of the way in which you live, you will produce all kinds of good deeds." The phrase all kinds of good deeds may be rendered as "you will do good in all different ways."

Your knowledge of God: God is the object of knowledge, not the the subject.

A verb meaning "grow" may seem to be very strange in combination with a phrase such as "your knowledge of God." What is meant here is simply an increase of knowledge, and therefore one may say "and you will know God more and more" or "your experience of God will be greater and greater."

1.11-12   May you be made strong with all the strength which
            comes from his glorious power, so that you may be
            able to endure everything with patience. And with
            joy give thanks to[b] the Father, who has made you fit
            to have your share of what God has reserved for his
            people in the kingdom of light.

            [b]with patience. And with joy give thanks to; or with
            patience and joy. And give thanks to.

The initial participial clause, "being empowered with all power according to the might of his glory," may be taken as a circumstantial clause, "as you are made strong," or absolutely (as participles in Greek New Testament often are) as a wish or a command (as "give thanks" in verse 12). This expression of Paul's wish for the believers in Colossae must be expressed in a number of languages as a type of prayer, for example, "I pray that you may be made strong." It may, however, be important to introduce God as agent, for example, "I pray that God will cause you to be strong."
    A literal rendering of be made strong with all the strength may seem quite strange and even unintelligible, but the real problem is involved in relating this increase of strength with his glorious power. The connection may be made by a restructuring, so as to translate "I pray that God by using his glorious power may cause you to be exceedingly strong." This strength, however, must not be understood in terms of physical strength or prowess. It is obviously related to the enduring of hardships with patience and therefore in some languages one must translate "strong in your spirits" or "strong in your hearts," for this is psychological strength and not physical strength.
    His glorious power (so most translations) is an inadequate translation of "the might of his glory," since the noun doxa almost always (as its Heb counterpart kābōd) represents the self-revelation of God as his presence with his people to save them. This characteristic of God is described in terms of light (compare Ex 16.10, 1 Kgs 8.10-11, Ezek 10.3-4). TC has "the power manifested in his Glory," Gpd "so mighty is his majesty," GeCL "his complete godly power and might." His glorious power may be rendered in some languages as "his power which is so wonderful" or even "the fact that he is so wonderfully powerful."
    Endure...with patience represents two nouns in Greek whose meanings overlap each other; "steadfastness" (hupomonē) occurs in the NT more often than "endurance" (makrothumia). TNT "stand firm and be patient," NEB Brc "fortitude and patience," Mft "endure and be patient," Gpd "endurance and forbearance."

[17]

In some instances, it may be essential to indicate the nature of what is to be endured, for example, "endure persecution" or "remain firm despite troubles." In some languages, patience is best expressed as a negation of some negative quality, for example, "enduring without complaining" or "enduring and not being resentful."

With joy may go with what precedes (so Lightfoot, Moule, RSV NEB Phps NAB Brc SpCL JB Mft Gpd) or with what follows (Abbott, TNT NIV). If the phrase with joy is to be related to what precedes, one may say "to endure persecution without complaining and with happiness" or "...while continuing to be happy." In a number of languages, joy is expressed figuratively, for example, "with a happy heart," or "with dancing in one's heart," or "with a heart that sings."

If the phrase with joy is to be combined with the giving of thanks, it is often possible to employ a coordinate phrase such as "be happy and give thanks."

Give thanks represents a participle, understood by TEV as an injunction or command, not as a circumstance ("as you give thanks") or as a participle of means, dependent on the main verb "to live" in verse 10, that is, "by giving thanks" (so NIV).

It is frequently impossible to speak of God as "the Father," since a kinship term such as "father" must be possessed, that is to say, a father is always the father of someone. In certain languages, the closest equivalent of the Father is "the father of us all." In other instances, it may be necessary to use an expanded phrase such as "God our father." It is important not to conclude that one can communicate the meaning of father in this context merely by a device such as capitalization. The Scriptures are heard far more widely than they are read, and obviously capitalization does not show up in pronunciation.

Has made you fit: the verb hikanoō is causative, to make someone hikanos, that is, fit, qualified, competent, sufficient (see the verb in 2 Cor 3.6; the noun in 2 Cor 3.5; and the adjective, in this sense, in 2 Cor 2.16, 3.5; 2 Tim 2.2). JB "made it possible for you"; NIV "qualified"; Gpd "entitled you"; Phps "you are privileged." In some languages, the concept of fit may be expressed as "cause you to be the kind of person who can share" or "cause you to be the type of person who is worthy to share."

In verse 12, RSV lists "us" as a variant reading (for "you"); "you" is the form better supported by external evidence; some commentators and translators, however, prefer us which, if adopted, is inclusive, meaning "all of us Christians."

Your share of what God has reserved for his people: the noun klēros "lot" means that which is allotted or assigned to someone; it is a biblical word whose meaning springs from its application to the Promised Land, as the territory allotted by God to the Israelites as their exclusive possession. It became a figure of all of God's blessings for his people, especially those reserved for the future; whence the use of "inherit eternal life," etc. The use in English of "inheritance" (so RSV, compare NEB JB NIV) is not recommended (compare TNT note), since it implies the transference of property as the result of the original owner's death.

Your share may be expressed as "what rightfully belongs to you" or literally "your part."

The clause of what God has reserved for his people may be expressed as "of what God has designated for his people," or "...set aside for his people," or even "...promised to give to his people."

His people: see 1.2.

In the kingdom of light represents the Greek "in the light." The clue for the use of kingdom comes from the next verse, and it (or "realm") is used here also by GeCL FrCL NIV Gpd Brc TNT TC. The kingdom of light is here a synonym for "the kingdom of God," with emphasis on "the light," that is, God's own life, which shines on God's people. Because of the extensive use of the figurative language for "light" and "darkness," it is important to preserve the figurative significance and not to adopt merely an equivalent such as "the kingdom of God." Some translators have employed a compromise expression such as "the kingdom of God, who is light" or even "the kingdom of God's light." At this point, it may be relevant to employ a footnote to identify the figurative significance of "light" versus "darkness," for the contrast is not a matter of knowledge versus ignorance but of (1) moral and ethical truth in contrast with sin and disobedience, and (2) life in contrast with death. In a number of languages, there are very distinct words for "light" depending upon the nature of the light: (1) general light as in the case of daylight; (2) the light which radiates from a particular source such as a torch or lamp; and (3) unusual forms of light, as in the case of the northern lights (aurora borealis). Even the light of day may be subdivided into different aspects, for example, dawn before sunrise, early morning, midday, late afternoon, and twilight. In general the term which identifies the bright light of the day has the potential for greatest generalization of meaning and therefore is usually to be preferred to terms which may suggest only partial light or light coming from a lamp or a fire.

1.13-14   13 He rescued us from the power of darkness and
           brought us safe into the kingdom of his dear
           Son, 14 by whom we are set free, that is, our
           sins are forgiven.

Verses 13-14 serve as a transition to the next section, by describing God's redemptive activity through Jesus Christ.

He rescued us: the verb ruomai is significantly appropriate here, in terms of the rescue of captives from an evil power, the power of darkness, a descriptive figure of the spiritual power by which mankind is held prisoner. It forcefully portrays the gracious initiative and independent activity of God, the impotence and helplessness of man, and the contrast between the two modes of existence. Us is here inclusive, of course, designating all who have been set free.

In place of the past tense forms rescued and brought, it may be important to use a perfective tense, for example, "he has rescued us" and "he has brought us." In this way, one may emphasize not only a past event but the continuing reality of such an experience.

"To be rescued from the power of darkness" may seem to be a very strange and almost impossible expression. A literal translation might

suggest only rescuing somebody who was lost in the darkness of night.
Sometimes the relationship between the realm of darkness and the kingdom
of light may be emphasized by saying "he rescued us from the dark realm
which had power over us," or "...the dark realm which controlled us," or
"...where we were tied down, as it were."

Brought us safe is literally "transferred, removed" (see the verb
methistēmi elsewhere in Luke 16.4, Acts 13.22, 19.26, 1 Cor 13.2).

The kingdom of his dear Son should not be understood as a geographical
place, but rather as a "rule" or "realm of authority." One may, therefore,
translate "brought us safe under the rule of his dear Son" (so GeCL) or
"brought us safe to the point where his dear Son rules over us." In verses
12,13, and 14, there is not only a good deal of specific figurative
language, but the entire passage has a figurative theme. In a sense, it
is the theme which provides clues to the use of the figurative language,
and therefore, in a sense, the very abundance of figurative expressions
tends to reinforce one another and, therefore, suggests to the reader that
the entire passage must be taken in a non-literal sense.

His dear Son may be rendered as "his Son whom he loves."

By whom or, as in RSV, "in whom," meaning "in union with whom"; the
idea of instrumentality, however, seems preferable here.

We are set free...our sins are forgiven are both verbal expressions
of what in Greek are nouns; "redemption and forgiveness." The Greek word
apolutrōsis has here no idea in it, as has been sometimes suggested, of
a ransom paid to someone for the freeing of the captive; it stresses the
result of the action of liberation. The second noun "forgiveness (of sins)"
is in apposition to the first one, that is, it explains what is meant by
this liberation (so JB NIV Mft NAB). Some, however, make the two parallel
(NEB Phps GeCL), and TNT reverses the two. Others see a dependent relation
here: Brc "the liberation which comes when our sins are forgiven"; compare
SpCL Gpd.

By whom we are set free may be changed from passive to active by
translating "he is the one who set us free," expressed literally in some
languages as "caused us to no longer be prisoners" or "caused us no longer
to be slaves." One may also employ an active form with both primary and
secondary agents: "through him God set us free" or "God set us free; he
did it through his Son."

It should be observed that the phrase "through his blood" after the
word "redemption" is found in some late manuscripts (compare KJV SpCL),
having been introduced here by copyists from the parallel passage in
Eph 1.7.

The explanatory phrase that is may be rendered as "that means," or
"that is the same as," or "that says."

In place of the passive expression our sins are forgiven, one may
employ an active phrase with God as the subject, for example, "God has
forgiven our sins" or "because of him God has forgiven our sins." Expressions for forgiveness are frequently figurative, for example, "has
wiped away," "has thrown away," "has caused to disappear," or "has turned
his back on," or "has lost from his mind."

TEV   (1.15-20)   RSV

THE PERSON AND WORK OF CHRIST

15 Christ is the visible like-ness of the invisible God. He is the first-born Son, superior to all created things. 16 For through him God created everything in heaven and on earth, the seen and the unseen things, including spiritual powers, lords, rulers, and authorities. God created the whole universe through him and for him. 17 Christ existed be-fore all things, and in union with him all things have their proper place. 18 He is the head of his body, the church; he is the source of the body's life. He is the first-born Son, who was raised from death, in order that he alone might have the first place in all things. 19 For it was by God's own de-cision that the Son has in him-self the full nature of God. 20 Through the Son, then, God decided to bring the whole uni-verse back to himself. God made peace through his Son's death on the cross and so brought back to himself all things, both on earth and in heaven.

15 He is the image of the in-visible God, the first-born of all creation; 16 for in him all things were created, in heaven and on earth, visible and invisible, whether thrones or dominions or principalities or authorities--all things were created through him and for him. 17 He is before all things, and in him all things hold together. 18 He is the head of the body, the church; he is the beginning, the first-born from the dead, that in everything he might be pre-eminent. 19 For in him all the fulness of God was pleased to dwell, 20 and through him to re-concile to himself all things whether on earth or in heaven, making peace by the blood of his cross.

There is much discussion about whether this "hymn" about the person and work of Christ (verses 15-20) is Paul's own creation or whether it existed independently and was used, or adapted, by Paul in this letter. Whatever the conclusion reached on this question, its practical implication for the translator is slight, since he is bound to try to express the meaning in terms and fashion consistent with its setting in Colossians. The practical matter of whether or not to use a poetic form and structure will depend on the effect of such a form on the readers. Some modern translations, such as GeCL TOB JB, do so. First the Son's nature and existence (verse 15) are described, followed by his role in Creation, and his continuing relation to the universe (verses 16-17). Then his relation to the Church is stated (verse 18a), followed by another statement of his supremacy, by virtue of his resurrection (verse 18b, c). The final statement has to do with the reconciliation of all creation through him, effected by God through Christ's sacrificial death on the cross (verses 19-20).

<u>1.15</u>   Christ is the visible likeness of the invisible God. He is the first-born Son, superior to all created things.

<u>Christ</u>: the Greek begins with the relative "who" which refers to Christ, of course; it may be preferable to say "the Son" (as GeCL) since that is the form of the nearest reference (verse 13).

<u>Visible likeness</u> translates the Greek word for "image." Christ is elsewhere spoken of as the "image" of God (2 Cor 4.4). Man is also said to be the image of God (compare LXX Gen 1.27 "and God made man; according to God's image he made him, male and female he made them"; 1 Cor 11.7; compare James 3.9). The thought is that, in Christ, man can see what God is like, his very nature and being. In this context, the emphasis is not on the exactness of the likeness, but on its visibleness. GeCL "in the Son the invisible God became visible for us"; Phps "the visible representation of the invisible God"; TNT "he in his own person shows us what the invisible God is like."

There are distinct dangers in translating "image" in a more or less literal manner, for it is likely to be interpreted as either an idol or and icon. Accordingly, a translation such as "likeness" or "to be just like" is far better.

The attributives <u>visible</u> and <u>invisible</u> must often be rendered as relative clauses qualifying the objects involved, for example, "Christ who can be seen" and "God who cannot be seen," though in speaking of Christ it may be necessary to use a past tense form to refer to his visibility during his life on earth, for example, "Christ could be seen." The first sentence of verse 15 may then be translated as "Christ is like God, but he could be seen, while God cannot be seen." If an active rather than a passive form is required, one may translate "Christ is like God, except that people could see Christ but no one can see God."

<u>The first-born Son, superior to all created things</u> represents a three-word phrase in Greek, "first-born of all creation." Translated literally (as RSV), it implies that Christ is included in the created universe, which is inconsistent with the context of the whole passage. The prefix <u>prōtos</u> "first" may be taken in a temporal sense: "he was born before all creation" or in a hierarchical sense, "the begotten One is superior to all creation." As Lightfoot and Moule suggest, possibly both are intended. (It should be made clear that "born" or "begotten" refers not to the birth of Jesus in Bethlehem, but to the relation of Jesus to God, as the eternal Son and heir of the heavenly Father. The use of the word "born" or "begotten" emphasizes the unique relationship between God and Jesus which is best expressed in terms of father and son; unlike all other human beings Jesus' relation to God is not expressed in terms of creature and creator.) GeCL stresses the first element "He is the Father's first-born Son; he already existed before all creation." Lightfoot paraphrases: "He is the Firstborn, and as the Firstborn, the absolute Heir and sovereign Lord, of all creation." TNT

"He takes precedence over all the created universe"; NEB "his is the primacy over all created things." First-born in this context does not imply there were others who were likewise "born" afterward; it is a term which stresses the position of Jesus as the heir of his heavenly Father.

The use of the second element tokos ("beget" or "bear") excludes Christ from the process of creation; he was not created first, but was born first. A possible translation is: "God's first Son (or heir) who existed before all creation and is superior to it." There are some problems involved in rendering literally the first-born Son, since any term such as "birth" or "to be born" would suggest Christ's birth on earth at Bethlehem. A literal translation might also give the impression of some kind of miraculous birth by which God the Father actually gave birth to his Son named Christ. Another complication involved in the use of a word such as "born" might suggest some kind of sexual relations between God the Father and "mother earth." Therefore, it seems far better to use some such expression as "God's first Son" and to explain the concept of being "first" in terms of having "existed before anything else was created." The superiority of Christ to all creation can sometimes be expressed as "he is more important than all that was created" or "he ranks higher than all created things."

1.16   For through him God created everything in heaven and on earth, the seen and the unseen things, including spiritual powers, lords, rulers, and authorities. God created the whole universe through him and for him.

For through him: the Greek "in" is probably instrumental (as "in whom" in verse 14), "by means of" (Gpd Phps "through"); Brc "the agent by whom"; but TNT Mft NIV have "by." But the preposition normally used to convey the meaning "through" is dia (as in the last line of this verse; compare Heb 1.2; John 1.3,10; 1 Cor 8.6). In light of this, some see "in him" here as the sphere in which creation took place; so Beare and Moule, who combine the two; "by means of him and within him." But this spatial concept is unusual, to say the least. It could be "in union with him," but this is not expressed in any translation.

The problem of primary and secondary agency expressed in the phrase through him God created everything must often be rather radically restructured to communicate the same set of relations. In some instances, this is best expressed by a set of causative relationships, for example, "God caused Christ to create everything." In other instances, the relationship is expressed by a somewhat idiomatic syntactic structure "God created everything; Christ did it." Some languages, however, prefer to introduce a secondary agency with the verb "to help," for example, "God created everything with Christ helping him." None of these expressions are to be taken in a strictly literal sense; they are only different ways in which one may refer to the primary agent and the secondary agent of an action.

Everything in heaven and on earth must be expanded, in some instances, to read "everything which exists in heaven and everything which exists on earth." A literal rendering of this expression might mean those things which exist at the same time both in heaven and on earth, which is obviously not the meaning of the Greek phrase.

In choosing an equivalent expression for everything, it is important not to restrict the meaning to inanimate objects, for as the rest of the sentence clearly indicates, the spiritual powers are regarded as having certain aspects of personality.

The seen and the unseen things may be rendered as "what can be seen and what cannot be seen" or "what people can see and what people cannot see."

The rest of the sentence (TEV) expresses the totality of creation, the whole universe, as we would say today, including all supernatural powers. Four terms are used in Greek with no precise distinction intended; see comparable lists in Rom 8.38; 1 Cor 15.24; Eph 1.21, 3.10, 6.12; Col 2.10,15; 1 Peter 3.22. They denote supernatural creatures, conceived of as angels (in their various ranks) in Jewish thought, or as lesser gods or powers, in Greek philosophy. In this passage, they are treated as existing and as morally neutral (whether good or bad is not in question), but they are included among created beings, that is, without independent existence apart from God. As with all other created beings, they are dependent on and subordinate to God.

A translation need not use four separate titles to describe these beings; compare GeCL "the unseen Powers and Authorities."

It may be practically impossible to translate literally spiritual powers, lords, rulers, and authorities. The term powers normally expresses a quality of something else while the adjective spiritual really refers to "spirit beings." It may, therefore, be important to reverse the attributive relationships and talk about "including spirits which are powerful, govern, rule, and exercise authority." In some instances, it may be important to indicate something of the realm in which such spirits function. Therefore, one may say "in the region between heaven and earth," since in ancient times such spirit beings were regarded as having their realm of authority over the earth.

The last sentence summarizes the thought of the first part of the verse. God created here represents the perfect passive of the verb, whereas in the first part of the verse, it is the aorist passive; it is possible that a distinction in meaning is intended, that is, "created" and "has created" (but see Turner Moulton III, 68-70). In both instances, the passive voice in Greek is used to express divine activity. The new element is for him (also Phps NIV TNT NEB JB NAB, etc.), which is not an entirely adequate representation of the preposition eis, which indicates purpose or goal. The whole line is better represented by Brc, "He is the agent and goal of all creation." That is, creation finds its purpose, its goal, its finality in Christ. GeCL "God has created everything through him, and everything has its goal in him."

The rendering of God created the whole universe through him must be expressed in essentially the same way as the similar statement at the beginning of verse 16. The phrase the whole universe may be rendered simply as "everything that exists" or, as in some languages, "the earth and the heavens."

The phrase for him may be simply rendered as "for his benefit." To

say literally that "everything has its goal in him" is extremely
difficult to express in some languages. One might approximate this
meaning by employing a phrase such as "Christ is the purpose for which
everything exists," but this likewise may be relatively meaningless.
Perhaps the closest equivalent would really be "the purpose of everything is to honor Christ."

1.17   Christ existed before all things, and in union
             with him all things have their proper place.

    He existed before all things: although the preposition pro could
indicate position, "superior to," it seems more likely that it is here
used temporally "before." It may be impossible to translate literally
Christ existed before all things, since it may be necessary to stipulate
Christ's having existed before other things came into existence, for example, "Christ existed before anything else existed" or "...before anything was created."
    And in union with him all things have their proper place is an
attempt to translate the verb sunistēmi, the only place in the NT where
it is used in this sense (except, perhaps, in 2 Peter 3.5). It carries
the idea of consistence, harmony, congruence; it represents the unifying
power, the integrating principle. NEB "all things are held together in
him"; GeCL "through him everything has stability." There is order and
harmony in all creation; it is a universe, not a chaos, and Christ is
the unifying force. Compare Wisdom 1.7: the Spirit of God is to sunechon
ta panta "what holds everything together/in harmony." Brc TNT NIV use
"hold together"; JB "he holds all things in unity." In order to identify
Christ as the unifying force of all creation, one may say "everything
fits together because of Christ" or "Christ is the one who causes everything to fit together." In some languages, the concept of "fitting
together" is related to the construction of furniture, so that a phrase
such as "everything remains in its place" may be appropriate or "everything is dovetailed together," in which the strongest and most effective
joint in carpentry is identified by "dovetailing."

1.18   He is the head of his body, the church; he is the
             source of the body's life. He is the first-born
             Son, who was raised from death, in order that he
             alone might have the first place in all things.

    From Christ's relation to creation, the thought now turns to his
relation to the Church, with the opening statement He is the head of his
body, the church. The idea of "head" is that of power, rule, authority
(see Eph 1.22-23). The metaphor "head of the body" represents the
supremacy of Christ and the unity of all Christians as a living organism
which belongs to Christ.
    A literal rendering of the statement He is the head of his body may
seem not only strange but even rather ludicrous. As a result, one may
wish to change the order of the expressions which are in apposition, namely his body and the church. The translation may then read "he is the head
of the church which is his body." In some languages, however, it is not

possible to use a term such as "head" to identify supremacy over or the governing of some object. One may have to say "he is the one who is supreme over the church, which is his body" or "he is the one who governs the church, which is his body."

He is the source of the body's life represents in Greek "he is the beginning" (or source). Two questions arise: (1) does this refer to creation or to the Church? Most prefer the latter; simply to say "he is the beginning" (RSV Phps NIV) is inadequate. (2) What relation with the Church does it designate? TNT "its founder"; Brc "its beginning"; GeCL "he is the source of the new life"; FrCL "it is in him that the new life begins"; TC "the Source of its Life." In favor of the idea "source of its life" is the belief, current at that time, that from the head came the life and nourishment that kept the body alive. But the variety of translations shows that no dogmatic certainty is possible.

There are certain serious problems involved in any literal translation of he is the source of the body's life, for this might very well suggest that Christ is the food which nourishes the body. The relationship may be expressed as causative, for example, "he is the one who causes the body to live."

The first-born Son, who was raised from death: for "first-born Son" see verse 15. The resurrection is perhaps referred to here as the reason why Christ is the source of the body's life: "because he was the first-born Son to rise from death." It is possible that born here refers specifically to the resurrection: so GeCL "the first who was returned from death"; Brc "for he was the first to return from the dead." But the use of prōtotokos (and not simply prōtos) makes it difficult to take the word as indicating only priority in time. FrCL combines the two: "he is the first-born Son, the first to have been brought back from death to life." Or, in line with Rom 1.4, it could be taken to mean "he is the first-born Son, as shown by his resurrection." (See the similar ho prōtotokos tōn nekrōn in Rev 1.5.)

If one translates first-born Son as "first Son," it is important to employ a qualifying statement such as "who was raised from death" which will be clearly non-restrictive. That is to say, one should not give the impression that Christ is simply "the first son who was raised from death," implying that other sons were also "raised from the dead." In order to avoid such a misunderstanding, one may often translate this phrase as "he is God's first son; God raised him from death." In a number of languages, however, one cannot speak of the resurrection as being simply "raised from death." The meaning must be formally restructured in some such manner as "God caused him to live again," or "God gave him back his life," or even "God caused his life to return to him."

Have the first place translates a verbal phrase "that he might become supreme, and it may be expressed as "be above all else," or "to have the preferred place," or "to have a place of commanding."

In all things: this could be "in every way" (so JB) or "among all people." But the context argues for the neuter "in all things." In all things may be better expressed in some languages as "over all things." A literal rendering of in all things might suggest merely "among all things."

1.19   For it was by God's own decision that the Son has
in himself the full nature of God.

     This verse continues as a justification of all that is said of
Christ in the preceding verse: "All this is true about him because..."
The meaning of what follows is disputed. The Greek may mean: God decided
to have his fullness dwell in Christ, or God's fullness decided to dwell
in Christ, depending on whether the neuter phrase pan to plērōma is con-
strued as an accusative, the object of the verb, or as nominative, the
subject of the verb. (1) Object: Lightfoot; NEB NAB NIV JB TNT Brc TOB
GeCL TC; (2) Subject: Abbott, Moule; Phps Mft Gpd. If taken as subject,
the rendition of it must somehow personify what is, linguistically, an
abstract concept, "all the fullness" (of God), which may be quite
difficult. To have, as RSV does, "in him all the fulness of God was
pleased to dwell," is not very satisfying.

     It seems better to take "all the fullness" as object, and God as
the (unexpressed) subject of the sentence: "it was God's choice/decision/
pleasure (for the verb eudokeō compare 1 Cor 1.21, Gal 1.15; compare the
noun eudokia in Eph 1.5,9; Phil 2.13) to have all the fullness dwell in
him." GeCL "It was God's will and plan."

     For it was by God's own decision may be expressed more simply as
"for God himself decided."

     The full nature of God represents the Greek "all the fullness."
The passive noun plērōma has been understood to mean either that which
fills or completes, or the resulting state of fullness, completion (compare John 1.16, Eph 1.23, 3.19, 4.13, Col 2.9). (If, as seems probable,
this word was being used by the false teachers in Colossae of the intermediary spiritual beings between God and creation, here it is used
deliberately to counter that false notion and to assert that in Christ
alone was the fullness of the divine nature, not interspersed among a
number of intermediary beings.) There are extensive discussions of the
word "fullness" in commentaries on Colossians and Ephesians. The view
favored here, and expressed by the majority of translations, is that it
means God's complete nature (see also 2.9), undiminished, undiluted, and
unshared with any "intermediaries" between God and creation. It seems
preferable to say "God's full nature lives/dwells in him" than to say
"God in his fullness dwells in him" (compare TNT Brc FrCL), as though
the person of God were exhausted by the incarnation.

     Has in himself represents the Greek katoikeō, "to live," "to be at
home" (oikos, "house," "home").

     A literal rendering of the Son has in himself the full nature of
God can lead to misunderstanding, for it might suggest that Christ simply
possessed God inside of himself. A more satisfactory equivalent in some
languages is "the son is just like God." A more elaborate way of expressing this meaning might be "what is characteristic of God is also
characteristic of God's Son" or "what makes God really God is also true
of his Son."

1.20   Through the Son, then, God decided to bring the whole
universe back to himself. God made peace through his
Son's death on the cross and so brought back to himself

all things, both on earth and in heaven.

Verse 20, in Greek, continues without a break from verse 19, the infinitive "to reconcile" (RSV) being governed by the main verb "he decided" in verse 19.

Bring...back to himself represents the Greek apokatallassō "to reconcile." Two things should be noted: (1) This implies a previous state of estrangement, of alienation; and what is explicitly said throughout the NT and implicit here is that creation (which, in biblical thought, includes animate and inanimate creation) has alienated itself, has separated itself from God. God is not himself estranged; he does not need reconciling. (2) It is God who takes the initiative; he, through his Son, effects the reconciliation; creation, sinful mankind, is the object of God's reconciling activity. (The compound verb apokatallassō occurs here and in the next verse, and Eph 2.16; the simple katallassō in Rom 5.10, 2 Cor 5.18-20; the noun katallagē in Rom 5.11, 11.15.)

As in the case of verse 16, the statement through the Son, then, God decided to bring indicates again both primary and secondary agency. An equivalent, in this context, may be "God decided to bring with the help of his Son."

The transitional particle then is not primarily temporal but suggests a conclusion, equivalent in some languages to "and so" or "accordingly."

There are a number of serious problems involved in trying to obtain a fully satisfactory expression for "reconcile." In some instances, seemingly acceptable expressions have proven to be misleading, since the individual who undertakes the process of reconciliation is often regarded as acknowledging his own fault or responsibility for the prior estrangement. Such a feature of meaning would, of course, be quite out of place in speaking of God reconciling the universe to himself through Christ. In some languages in Africa, it is appropriate to use a term for reconciliation which is normally used in speaking of the reconciliation of a husband and wife, since it is usually taken for granted that it is the wife's fault for any estrangement. Other problems to be considered in obtaining a satisfactory expression for reconciliation may involve a feature of mutual blame of estrangement, and this inevitably causes problems for the use of such an expression in this type of context. Accordingly, it may be far more appropriate to use some phrase rather than a traditional term, since such terms often acquire highly specific connotations of meaning in view of local usage.

To bring the whole universe back to himself may be expressed in some languages as "to cause the whole universe to return to himself" or in an idiomatic fashion "to cause the whole universe to be friendly with him again." In some instances, the relationship must be expressed as a willingness to accept control, for example, "decided to cause the whole universe to welcome his control again." Such "control" must not imply mere physical control but a change from a state of alienation. Sometimes the statement on reconciliation itself may be expressed negatively in terms of alienation, for example, "God decided to cause the whole universe no longer to be alienated from himself."

The whole universe is simply, as often in this passage, "all things" (verses 16,17), further defined in the last part of the verse as "both the things on earth and the things in heaven."

To himself that is to God. Although printed in the Greek text <u>eis</u> <u>auton</u> "to him" (which could mean "to Christ"), nearly all commentaries and translations are agreed that God is meant (exceptions: TOB Mft JB NAB). See Moule <u>Idiom Book</u>, 119. The reconciliation was effected by means of the peace which God brought about <u>through his Son's death on the cross</u>. The Greek is literally "through the <u>blood of his cross</u>." There have been strong objections to the use of the word "death" to represent the Greek "blood"; the principles of a dynamic equivalent translation, however, require some such wording: compare Phps "Christ's death on the cross," Brc "his death on the cross," also FrCL SpCL; GeCL, however, "through the blood that the Son sacrificed on the cross," NEB "through the shedding of his blood upon the cross" (where the "his" is ambiguous, as in NIV "through his blood, shed on the cross"). The <u>peace</u> that God made is the restoration of that fellowship between God and mankind which is broken by sin.

A literal rendering of <u>God made peace</u> can lead to misunderstanding, since it could be understood as God bringing together certain warring factions. What is referred to here is the process of reconciliation, and therefore, it may be best to render the first part of this second sentence in verse 20 as "God accomplished this through his Son's death on the cross."

The means expressed by the phrase <u>through his Son's death on the cross</u> must be expressed in a number of languages as cause, for example, "his Son died on the cross and this caused the peace" or "...caused the reconciliation." The relationship may also be expressed by some such rendering as "God made peace by means of the fact that his Son died on the cross."

Since <u>the cross</u> has not been previously mentioned in this discourse, it may in some languages be necessary to use an indefinite rather than a definite article, for example, "his Son died on a cross."

The last part of verse 20 simply summarizes what has already been said about reconciliation of everything, made somewhat more explicit by the final phrase <u>both on earth and in heaven</u>, but as in verse 16 it may be necessary to indicate "all those things on earth and all those things in heaven."

<table>
<tr><td>TEV</td><td>(1.21-23)</td><td>RSV</td></tr>
</table>

21 At one time you were far away from God and were his enemies because of the evil things you did and thought. 22 But now, by means of the physical death of his Son, God has made you his friends, in order to bring you, holy, pure, and faultless, into his presence. 23 You must, of course, continue faithful on a firm and sure foundation, and must not allow

21 And you, who once were estranged and hostile in mind, doing evil deeds, 22 he has now reconciled in his body of flesh by his death, in order to present you holy and blameless and irreproachable before him, 23 provided that you continue in the faith, stable and steadfast, not shifting from the hope of the gospel which you heard, which has been preached to

yourselves to be shaken from the hope you gained when you heard the gospel. It is of this gospel that I, Paul, became a servant--this gospel which has been preached to everybody in the world.

every creature under heaven, and of which I, Paul, became a minister.

On the basis of what he has said about the person and work of Christ, Paul now shows the effect of that on his readers in one long sweeping statement that goes without a full stop to the end of verse 23. He states, in an dependent clause, their previous condition before knowing Christ (verse 21), followed by the main verb "he has reconciled" (verse 22), which describes God's saving act and its purpose ("in order to..."), whose fulfillment is conditioned by the constancy and faithfulness of the Colossians in adhering to the gospel preached by Paul to them (verse 23). The mention of his role in the spread of the gospel forms the bridge linking this section to the following one.

1.21   At one time you were far away from God and were his enemies because of the evil things you did and thought.

A literal rendering of at one time might very well suggest that on a particular occasion, but not necessarily for any period of time, the believers in Colossae were estranged from God. The meaning here is simply "previously," or "before you became believers," or "before you put your trust in Christ."
Paul begins the sentence with an accusative clause before the main verb (God has made you his friends, in verse 22) in order to emphasize his readers' previous condition before hearing the gospel. They had been far away from God, that is, estranged or alienated from him. The compound verb apallotrioō is found only here and Eph 2.12, 4.18; it is formed from the adjective allotrios "stranger," "foreigner" (see Matt 17.25-26, Heb 11.9), and refers to their condition as Gentiles, not part of God's people, Israel (see the fuller statement of this in Eph 2.11-12). The passive participle simply states their condition, without giving its cause.
A literal translation of you were far away from God may very well be interpreted in a strictly literal sense, since earth is presumably far away from heaven, so the believers in Colossae were obviously far away from God. This estrangement from God must not, however, be expressed as "you were strangers to God" for this would imply that God did not recognize who they were. The responsibility for the estrangement must be expressed in terms of the actions or attitudes of the people, not the attitude of God. Thus it may be better to say "you were estranged from God," or "you had turned your back on God," or "you did not want to be friends with God."
Not only were these believers previously far away from God, but both in thought and actions, they showed themselves to be God's enemies. This word denotes their hostility toward God (compare TNT "your thinking was all against him"), not his attitude toward them. They had been enemies

"in thinking, in evil works." "Thinking" (TEV you...thought) is the
Greek dianoia "mind," "understanding" (compare Eph 2.3, 4.18, 1 Peter
1.13, 2 Peter 3.1, 1 John 5.20); in LXX it often represents Hebrew lev
"heart." "Evil works" are sinful, wicked action. These phrases are in the
dative case, and their precise relationship to enemies is not explicitly
stated by any connectives. The meaning is expressed in various ways: Gpd
"hostile in attitude," Phps "his spiritual enemies." TOB "you whose evil
deeds manifested profound hostility." TEV sees cause as the relationship,
because of the evil things (see also Phps NIV TNT), but other interpretations are possible: JB "in the way that you used to think," Brc and NEB
take them as simply descriptive of the estrangement (so Lightfoot), and
this may be the best way to handle this phrase; NEB "you were his enemies
in heart and mind, and your deeds were evil."
    A statement such as "you were his enemies" can be misleading, for
it might suggest that God was hostile to the people of Colossae. It may,
therefore, be necessary to say "you were fighting against God" or "you
made yourselves enemies of God."
    Because of the evil things you did and thought may be better ex-
pressed in many instances by indicating means, for example, "you were
fighting against God by means of the evil things you did and the evil
thoughts that you had." In some instances, the evil things you did and
thought may be rendered as "what you did and thought which was evil."

1.22   But now, by means of the physical death of his Son,
            God has made you his friends, in order to bring you,
            holy, pure, and faultless, into his presence.

    Here Paul describes their present status with a sharp contrastive
phrase: but now, followed by the verb "to reconcile" (see verse 20). The
textual evidence is divided over whether the verb is active indicative
third singular "he (God) reconciled (you)," or a passive participle "you
having been reconciled," or a passive second plural indicative "you have
been reconciled." The hardest reading is the participle; as the United
Bible Societies Textual Commentary says, the majority of the Committee
considered "a passive participle to be totally unsuitable in the context." The 2nd edition of the UBS Greek New Testament had the passive
indicative in the text, but in the 3rd edition the text has the active
indicative "he has reconciled." For the translation, the textual problem
does not present a very great difficulty; and in most cases, it will be
preferable to represent the meaning by using the verb in the active
voice, not the passive. The subject of the verb is probably to be taken
as God, who is spoken of as the actor in the work of reconciliation,
with Christ as the agent through whom God effects the reconciliation,
that is, God has made you his friends. However, NAB Gpd Mft make Christ
the subject of the verb.
    The process of reconciliation is often expressed in figurative
language, even as it is in the English figure of speech God has made you
his friends. In other languages, the process of reconciliation may be
described as "he has tied you together again," or "he has brought you
together to snap fingers" (in certain parts of Africa snapping fingers
together is equivalent to shaking hands), or "he has caused you to cut

your differences."

By means of the physical death of his Son represents what is literally "by the body of his flesh through the death," which quite clearly means what TEV says. The reference is to the death of Christ, not of God, and a translation must make that explicit. The phrase "the body of flesh" appears again in 2.11; as Moule points out, it may be that this phrase stresses not only the physical body of Christ (as contrasted with the Church as his spiritual body, verse 18) but the reality of his physical death. TNT translates "through his Son, who lived and died," Brc, more felicitously, "by the incarnation and death of his Son," NEB "by Christ's death in his body of flesh and blood," GeCL "But because his Son died as a human being, God has accepted you as his friends."

In a number of languages, there are problems involved in making clear the distinction between means and cause. If one translates by means of the physical death of his Son as "because his Son really died," this might suggest only a reason which prompted God to do something, not the means by which God effected a particular result. Sometimes means must be expressed essentially as a cause, but it should be a so-called "effective cause" and not merely a reason, for example, "God's son died and this has made possible God's making you his friends" or even "God has used the fact that his son died to make you his friends."

(In order) to bring you...into his presence: as translated by TEV, God is the subject of the verb and his refers to God; so also the translations that make God the subject of "he reconciled." Those that make Christ the subject of "he reconciled," also make him the subject of "to present" and take "before him," as a reference to God. The Greek "to present you" may be understood as transitive, with God (or Christ) as subject, and "you" as object; or it may be understood intransitively, meaning "(for) you to stand." Most understand it as transitive, but JB takes it as intransitive ("now you are able to appear before him"); and GeCL takes it as an imperative, "Stand before him." The language is that of an offering or sacrifice (compare such use of the verb in this kind of context in Luke 2.22, Rom 12.1, Eph 5.27, Col 1.28); it may seem odd to say that God "presents" a gift, or offering to himself (but see also Eph 5.27). Most translators take the infinitive to express purpose, as do RSV and TEV, in order to; JB, however, takes it to represent result. This "presentation" is probably thought of as an eschatological event, when all will be brought into his presence.

To bring you...into his presence may be rendered as a causative, for example, "to cause you to stand before him" or "to cause you to be where he is."

The three adjectives holy, pure, and faultless describe moral and spiritual qualities (in Greek there is a rhetorical effect, achieved through alliteration; all three begin with the letter alpha). No precise and discrete areas of meaning are to be sought for each separate adjective; the three are used for effect, to denote complete and total purity, the effect of Christ's redemptive death in purifying his people from all their sins, blemishes, and faults.

Since the three adjectives holy, pure, and faultless serve primarily to intensify the concept of being without blame, this may be expressed in some languages by using qualifying expressions, for example, "completely without blame in any way," or "completely without the slightest amount of guilt," or "not having guilt for anything at all." This somewhat negative way of speaking of something which is holy and pure is not at all unusual. These adjectives which are positives in English are more often than not expressed negatively in other languages; that is to say, the focus is upon the absence of something bad rather than some positive quality.

1.23   You must, of course, continue faithful on a firm and sure foundation, and must not allow yourselves to be shaken from the hope you gained when you heard the gospel. It is of this gospel that I, Paul, became a servant--this gospel which has been preached to everybody in the world.

Without a full stop, Paul qualifies the statement made in verse 22, since it is imperative that the Colossians recognize that they are not just passive objects of God's reconciling work, but must actively do their part in maintaining the state in which they now find themselves. In effect he says, "this is true if you continue..." This type of contrast between the contents of verse 23 and verse 22 may also be expressed as "but you must certainly continue."

Faithful translates the dative "(in) the faith," and some (RSV Mft Phps JB) take it as reference to the Christian faith, that is, "in your faith" (Lightfoot, Abbott; see NIV NEB Brc TNT). NAB "hold steadfast to faith," TOB par la foi, presumably, "by means of the faith," Gpd "the exercise of faith." The implied object of faithful is probably "the gospel"; it is not likely that here the primary reference would be God or Christ. In view of the fact that in so many languages it is necessary to make explicit what is the goal or object of "faith," one may, in this instance, say "continue to put your trust in the good news" or "continue to have confidence in the gospel."

On a firm and sure foundation translates a perfect passive participle "having been placed and remaining on a foundation" (as in Eph 3.17; see the verb also in Matt 7.25), followed by the adjective "firm, steadfast." The foundation is to be understood as the mighty work of God in salvation, as proclaimed by the gospel.

Though the figurative expression of foundation is readily perceived and understood in the cultures of western Europe, America, and some parts of Asia, this is not true of many other regions in the world, where houses normally do not have foundations, and there seems nothing especially "firm and sure" about a foundation. One can use a type of simile with an expanded phrase such as "as it were, on something on which a house is built" but this becomes both awkward and often meaningless. It may be better in many cases to drop the figure of foundation and use merely "continue to have confidence in the gospel and thus be firm and secure." In some languages, an equivalent metaphor is to be found in expressions relating to the central pole of a house, for example, "as unmovable as the central pole." Other languages may use the figure of a stone consisting essentially of bedrock, that is to say, stone which is part of a rock outcrop. One might, therefore, substitute a metaphor such as "firm and secure as bedrock."

Since such a metaphor parallels substantially the concept of foundation, it may be quite appropriate.

Again, there is no point in trying to determine who is the actor in this "foundation laying"; the participle, acting as an adjective, simply means "on a firm foundation." The thought is further expressed in the negative form and not allow yourselves to be shaken from. The verb (which occurs only here in the NT) means "to remove from"; TEV and others (Phps NIV NEB TOB) take it as a passive, but it may be understood as a middle: Mft "instead of shifting from," Gpd "and never shift from," TC "never abandoning," TNT "do not shift from," JB "never letting yourselves drift away."

To be shaken is in evident contrast with being firm, but it may be extremely difficult to understand the relationship between to be shaken and hope. Therefore, it may be necessary to say "you must not permit yourselves to be shaken and thus no longer to have the hope" or "...to lose your hope."

"The hope of the gospel" (RSV) is the hope the gospel brings to those who believe it, that is, of God's full and final deliverance in the future. JB "the hope promised by the Good News." The hope you gained when you heard the gospel may be expressed as "the hope that became yours when you heard the gospel." However, if hope must be expressed as a verb, then it may be possible to say "to be shaken and hence no longer hope as you did when you heard the gospel."

Having mentioned the gospel, Paul says two things about it: (1) "it has been preached to every creature under heaven" (RSV), a biblical way of saying to everybody in the world, which is, of course, a rhetorical statement not to be taken literally; it speaks simply of the widespread dissemination of the gospel throughout the Roman Empire. Gpd "all over the world," TNT "through the whole world," JB "the whole human race." The verb "to preach" is the one used normally in the NT to describe the proclamation of the Good News. No word should be used which, like "preach" in English, suggests a formal church service; the verb means "to announce," "to proclaim" as a herald who went around announcing matters of importance. (2) Paul says also of the gospel, "I became its servant" (see also Eph 3.7, 2 Cor 3.6).

Despite the exaggeration suggested in the literary figure which has been preached to everybody in the world, it is important to reflect, in so far as possible, this type of statement made by Paul. However, the passive expression must often be changed into an active one, and this means introducing an agent, for example, "this gospel which various persons have announced to everyone in the world." It would be inappropriate to introduce "apostles," since obviously a great deal of the spreading of the gospel was performed by other persons. Therefore, some kind of indefinite subject is preferable.

The word servant (diakonos) in Colossians (also in 1.7,25; 4.7) usually describes a relationship with a person or with God, or with an organization, such as the church (see 1.24-25, below); rarely is it used, as here, with an impersonal object (compare 2 Cor 3.6 "servants of the new covenant," Gal 2.17 "servant of sin," 1 Peter 1.12 the prophets "were serving" the news about the Messiah's suffering and glory). Paul characterizes his work as that of serving the gospel, meaning that his work was that of proclaiming, spreading, announcing the Good News. The noun "minister" (Mft Phps NEB) in American English may be misunderstood as a person ordained to an ecclesiastical position. In view of the unusual relationship between servant and gospel, it may be necessary to specify the precise relationship as "my work has been to announce this gospel" or perhaps "my task as a servant has been to proclaim this good news."

<table>
<tr><td>TEV</td><td>(1.24--2.5)</td><td>RSV</td></tr>
</table>

PAUL'S WORK AS A SERVANT OF
THE CHURCH

24 And now I am happy about my sufferings for you, for by means of my physical sufferings I am helping to complete what still remains of Christ's sufferings on behalf of his body, the church. 25 And I have been made a servant of the church by God, who gave me this task to perform for your good. It is the task of fully proclaiming his message, 26 which is the secret he hid through all past ages from all mankind but has now revealed to his people. 27 God's plan is to make known his secret to his people, this rich and glorious secret which he has for all peoples. And the secret is that Christ is in you, which means that you will share in the glory of God. 28 So we preach Christ to everyone. With all possible wisdom we warn and teach them in order to bring each one into God's presence as a mature individual in union with Christ. 29 To get this done I toil and struggle, using the mighty strength which Christ supplies and which is at work in me. 2 Let me tell you how hard I have worked for you and for the people in Laodicea and for all others who do not know me personally. 2 I do this in order that they may be drawn together in love, and so

24 Now I rejoice in my sufferings for your sake, and in my flesh I complete what is lacking in Christ's afflictions for the sake of his body, that is, the church, 25 of which I became a minister according to the divine office which was given to me for you, to make the word of God fully known, 26 the mystery hidden for ages and generations[c] but now made manifest to his saints. 27 To them God chose to make known how great among the Gentiles are the riches of the glory of this mystery, which is Christ in you, the hope of glory. 28 Him we proclaim, warning every man and teaching every man in all wisdom, that we may present every man mature in Christ. 29 For this I toil, striving with all the energy which he mightily inspires within me. 2 For I want you to know how greatly I strive for you, and for those at Laodicea and for all who have not seen my face, 2 that their hearts may be encouraged as they are knit together in love, to have all the riches of assured understanding and the knowledge of God's mystery, of Christ, 3 in whom are hid all the treasures of wisdom and knowledge. 4 I say this in order that no one may delude you with beguiling speech. 5 For though I am absent in body, yet I am with

have the full wealth of assurance which true understanding brings. In this way they will know God's secret which is Christ himself.[c] He is the key that opens all the hidden treasures of God's wisdom and knowledge.

4 I tell you, then, do not let anyone deceive you with false arguments, no matter how good they seem to be. 5 For even though I am absent in body, yet I am with you in spirit, and I am glad as I see the resolute firmness with which you stand together in your faith in Christ.

[c]God's secret, which is Christ himself; some manuscripts have God's secret; others have the secret of God the Father of Christ; others have the secret of the God and Father, and of Christ.

you in spirit, rejoicing to see your good order and the firmness of your faith in Christ.

[c]Or from angels and men

Having called himself "a servant of the gospel" (1.23), Paul writes at greater length about himself and the message he preaches (1.24-27). He then speaks of his work on behalf of the Colossians and others (1.28--2.3), and warns his readers against those who would lead them astray (2.4-5). This whole section is probably to be understood in the light of the false doctrines being taught in Colossae. It is clear that these false teachers are not Jewish, and that the issue is not the demand that Christians submit to the ritual demands of the Law of Moses but to the speculations of Greek teachers. So the attack centers on the adequacy of Paul's message, and not on his personal qualifications as an apostle. He counters with the statement that it was God who commissioned him (1.25), and that he does his work by means of God's power (1.29). He stresses his sufferings and his toil (1.29), and describes his commission as that of fully proclaiming God's message (1.25), the secret which has now been revealed (1.26-27) and which is to be found in Christ (2.2-3). Paul discharges his commission by preaching Christ to everyone, warning and teaching everyone with all wisdom (1.28). And even though he does not know the Colossians personally, he is concerned and feels responsible for them also (2.4-5).

1.24   And now I am happy about my sufferings for you,
           for by means of my physical sufferings I am helping
           to complete what still remains of Christ's suffer-
           ings on behalf of his body, the church.

Paul speaks of his sufferings on behalf of the Colossians, which can be understood only in a general sense of his hardships and troubles in his work as the apostle to the Gentiles, since he has had no personal contact with the Christians in Colossae.

Since the relationship between sufferings and being happy is essentially one of cause and effect, it may be important to make this quite explicit, for example, "my sufferings on your behalf have caused me to be happy" or "I am happy that I may now suffer for you." This may be far more meaningful than to say "happy about my sufferings."

By means of my physical sufferings may be expressed in some languages by a clause introduced by "because," for example, "because I suffer in my body" or simply "because I am suffering," in which case a verb for "suffering" should indicate physical suffering.

Now...my sufferings denotes his situation as a prisoner (4.10,18).

The relationship between Paul's sufferings and what still remains of Christ's sufferings is not easily understood. I am helping to complete translates a double compound verb (antanapleroō), found only here in the NT. The simple verb pleroō means "fill, fulfill," and the single compound anapleroō is an emphatic form, "fill completely." The added preposition anti "in the place of" or "on behalf of" indicates that this is done in the place of or on behalf of someone else. So here it means "complete, on Christ's behalf" or "in the place of Christ."

The expression Christ's sufferings may be understood more in a qualitative than in a literal sense; that is to say, these are "the kinds of suffering which Christ endured." In this way, one may avoid the impression that what Christ suffered was inadequate for atonement. One may, therefore, translate I am helping to complete what still remains of Christ's sufferings as "I am helping to complete the suffering which must be endured in the way Christ suffered" or "there is much suffering which people must endure and I am suffering in the way in which Christ suffered in order to complete the suffering which is necessary."

Christ's sufferings: the Greek for sufferings is here a different word from the one Paul uses for his own sufferings; it is possible that this word (thlipsis) was a technical term for the "tribulation" of the Messianic era, which would precede the end. What still remains translates a plural noun, literally, "the things lacking," "the deficiencies," and the plural, as such, states that there are sufferings still to be endured by Christ. In no sense, does Paul mean that Christ's suffering and death for the redemption of mankind was not sufficient; what is meant is that in the service of Christ his servants are called upon to suffer as he did; suffering is an integral part of the ministry of Christ's servants, as it was of Christ himself. Brc translates "the uncompleted sufferings which the work of Christ still entails."

Paul's sufferings are physical (lit. "in the flesh"), and they are on behalf of the church. There are two different ways of construing the phrase: (1) Paul's physical sufferings are on behalf of the church: RSV TC NIV TNT NEB GeCL; (2) Christ's sufferings are on behalf of the church: TEV Mft Gpd Phps JB NAB. Although it is impossible to state dogmatically which is intended, it seems more probable that the former is meant. It should be mentioned that some commentators and translations connect the phrase "in my flesh" to the immediately preceding "the afflictions of Christ"; they take this to mean that the afflictions of Christ are in the body of Paul; so Abbott; Mft "all that Christ has to suffer in my body," and as an alternative rendering in TOB; this, however, does not seem very probable.

If one wishes to make clear that it is Paul's suffering in this context which is on behalf of the church, it may be necessary to introduce a separate clause, for example, "this suffering of mine is on behalf of the church, which is Christ's body."

For his body, the church, see verse 18.

1.25   And I have been made a servant of the church by God,
                  who gave me this task to perform for your good. It
                  is the task of fully proclaiming his message,

Paul calls himself a servant of the church, using the same word for "servant" as in verse 23. In this context, the term servant may be rendered in some languages by a verb meaning "to help," for example, "I have been made a person to help the church." This passive form must in many languages, however, be changed into an active one, for example, "God has made me to be one who helps the church."

By the time a translator undertakes to translate the Epistle to the Colossians, he will most certainly have met with a number of problems related to determining a satisfactory word for translating the church as a collective. Obviously, in this context, as well as in other contexts in the Epistle to the Colossians, the church is not to be understood as a particular church but as the sum of all true believers. In some languages, the only appropriate equivalent for church is "those who worship Jesus" or "the worshipers of Christ," thus suggesting not only those who may be followers of the Lord, but those who gather together for worship. In the context of verse 25, there is always the possibility of people interpreting the "church" as being only the specific church in Colossae, and therefore some more general expression may be required. In some cases, it is necessary to use instead of a singular "the church" a plural expression "the churches," for only by means of a plural can the universality of the church of Christ be indicated.

He was made a servant (lit.) "according to God's stewardship which was given me." The Greek oikonomia means a position of responsiblity, an office, a task to perform. TNT "he entrusted a special task to me," NAB NIV "the commission God gave me," NEB "the task assigned to me by God," Mft Phps "divine commission," Gpd "divine appointment," TC "the office... which God entrusted me." (The word is used also in 1 Cor 9.17, Eph 3.2; for the cognate noun oikonomos see 1 Cor 4.1.) God appointed Paul to this position of trust for the benefit of the Colossians, for your good, that is, for their spiritual well being, their spiritual progress.

It is rare that one can translate literally who gave me this task to perform for tasks are not normally "given" but "assigned" or even "commanded." One may, however, often translate "he appointed me for this work" or "he pointed me out to do this work." The phrase for your good may be rendered as "in order to help you."

It is likely that Paul sees the Colossians as representatives of the Gentiles as a whole, since Paul had not been directly involved with them. The particular task God gave him was that of fully proclaiming his message. The construction is unusual, since fully proclaiming (RSV "make ...fully known") represents the Greek verb plēroō, which means "fill" or "fulfill." The nearest parallel is Rom 15.19, where the verb has "the gospel of Christ" as object; see also Col 4.17, "finish the task." It means to discharge fully, completely, the particular task, here defined as "(proclaiming) the word of God." This implies not simply the geographical extension of the task, but the thoroughness with which it is done. Mft "a full presentation of God's message," NEB "to deliver his message in full."

As already noted, the adverb fully may relate to the process of proclaiming and thus "complete my task of proclaiming," or it may be related to the nature of the message so that one may translate "to proclaim the complete message," or "to announce all the words of his message," or "to proclaim all that he has said."

1.26   which is the secret he hid through the past ages from all mankind but has now revealed to his people.

The message is called the secret he hid...but has now revealed. This "secret" or "mystery" is succinctly defined by J.A. Robinson (Ephesians) as "something that could not be known by men except by divine revelation, but that, though once hidden, has now been revealed in Christ and is to be proclaimed so that all who have ears may hear it." (See especially Rom 16.25, 1 Cor 2.1, 4.1, Eph 3.3,9; 6.19.) Lightfoot: "a truth which was once hidden but now is revealed." The content of this secret truth is given at the end of verse 27.

It is normally possible to speak of "hiding an object" but difficult, if not impossible, to "hide a secret." Futhermore, the term secret is often translated as "that which is not known" or "something which has not been told." Accordingly, one may translate which is the secret he hid as "which is something which he kept people from knowing," or "which he did not let people know about," or "which he did not tell people about."

This secret was hidden through all past ages from all mankind, (lit.) "from the ages and from the generations." RSV alternative rendering "from angels and men" is possible, since aiōn may be used to refer to the heavenly powers (as the singular is used in Eph 2.2). See the note in TNT. It seems likely that the two passives hid and revealed imply God as the actor: he hid (in the past) and he has revealed (now). For his people see 1.2.

Through all past ages may be expressed as "during all the time that is past," or "during all the years that are no longer," or "during all the days up to now." In a number of languages, there is simply no equivalent for ages. One can, of course, describe ages as "successive long periods of time," but in this context such an expression is not necessary.

From all mankind may be best expressed in close relationship to the verb hid, for example, "God kept all people from knowing."

Since the secret involved was something which is communicated by

words, one may translate has now revealed to his people as "has now told
it to his people" or "has now spoken about it to his people." One could
also use a verb such as "show," for example, "but he has now shown this
to his people."

1.27   God's plan is to make known his secret to his people,
          this rich and glorious secret which he has for all
          peoples. And the secret is that Christ is in you, which
          means that you will share in the glory of God.

The sentence, begun in verse 24, continues without a break, "to
whom (that is, to God's people) God willed to make known..." TEV and
others make a full break and start a new sentence. God's plan is translates
a verb "to plan," "to will," "to purpose," any of which carry the meaning;
care must be taken, however, not to translate in such a way as to imply
that God only "planned" or "purposed" to do it, without actually doing
it. In place of God's plan, it is possible to speak of "God's desire" or
"God's wish." The use of the present tense is is preferable in that this
represents not only what God has done, but what he continues to wish to
do. The first clause may be translated as "God desires to have his people
know what he hasn't made known before."
     To make known...this rich and glorious secret: the causative "to
make known" is equivalent in meaning to revealed in the previous verse.
In Greek the direct object is in the form of an indirect question, "what
(is) the wealth of the glory of this mystery," a biblical construction
employing genitive phrases where in English one more naturally uses
nouns and adjectives. It is hard to determine precisely what the phrase
"the wealth of the glory" means in this passage, since it is rather in-
congruous to attribute "wealth" and "glory" to a secret. Translations
handle the phrase (also in Rom 9.23, Eph 1.18, 3.16) in various ways:
NIV "the glorious riches," Mft "the glorious wealth," Phps "the wonder
and splendor of his secret plan." Perhaps something like "how magnificent
and splendid the secret is" or "the inexhaustible wonder contained in this
secret" achieves something of the effect intended.
     Since it is the content of the secret which is rich and glorious
rather than the fact of its being unknown, it may be best to make the
attributives rich and glorious apply to the content, for example, "how
rich and glorious is the truth which he has not revealed before" or "how
rich and wonderful is what he has not previously made known." Rather than
attempt to use two different adjectives such as "rich" and "glorious,"
it may be better in some languages to use a term such as "wonderful" and
employ an attributive so as to emphasize the importance or grandeur of
the secret, "how truly wonderful is the message which has not previously
been known!"
     Which he has for all peoples represents the Greek "in/among the
Gentiles." TNT is like RSV, "God's plan is to show his people how rich
and glorious this secret is among the Gentiles." While the translation
is defensible, it would seem that the Greek does not intend to say that
"the secret already exists among the Gentiles or is already known by them,
and that God's plan consists in making it known to his people." It would

seem rather to indicate that the scope of God's plan encompasses all mankind. The relevance of the contents of the secret for all peoples may be
expressed as "this applies to all people," or "this message concerns all
people," or "...is for the benefit of all peoples," or even "people
speaking all different languages," since a reference to different languages
is often a means by which different kinds of people can be identified.

The content of "the secret" is literally "Christ in you, the hope
of glory" (RSV). The preposition en could mean "among," that is Christ is
present with the believers, but "in" seems preferable: "Christ is in you."
As often in the NT, "hope" is more than an uncertain expectation; it is
assurance, confidence. TEV has expressed this assurance by use of a statement of fact; Gpd has "promise," FrCL "he gives you the assurance," GeCL
"you can depend on it that God gives you a share of his glory."

The secret is that Christ is in you may be rendered as "what hasn't
been known before is that Christ is in you," but to express in you in a
meaningful form one must often say "dwells in your hearts." If the meaning
is to be interpreted merely as "among you," then one may say "Christ
continues, as it were, to live among you."

If one wishes to emphasize the assurance which is involved in the
Greek term for "hope," it is possible to introduce the last clause of
verse 27 as "you may be sure that you will share."

In rendering share, it is so easy to introduce the wrong meaning,
for one can speak of "sharing the glory" as meaning distributing the glory
to others or as obtaining one's own part in the glory. It is this latter
meaning which is to be understood in this context; therefore, "you will
have your share in."

It is impossible to state dogmatically the precise content of glory
in this passage. The basic idea of the word is God's saving presence with
his people (see 1.11); here it refers to the eschatological fulfillment
of God's promise to live among his people, who will share in his might,
majesty, power, triumph; or, in a general way, as Phps has it, "all the
glorious things to come."

A literal translation of share in the glory of God might suggest
that God's glory is actually distributed to the believer and that accordingly
God ends up with much less glory than he had before. One way this problem
can be handled is to translate share in the glory of God as "caused by
God to become wonderful just as God is wonderful."

1.28   So we preach Christ to everyone. With all possible wisdom
          we warn and teach them in order to bring each one into
          God's presence as a mature individual in union with Christ.

Again Paul reverts to the task he and his colleagues perform: it is
that of "announcing" or "proclaiming" Christ; the verb here (kataggellō)
is different from the verb in 1.23 (kērussō), but describes the same
activity (compare its use in 1 Cor 2.1, 9.14, Phil 1.17). In a number of
languages, one cannot speak literally of "preaching Christ"; one can of
"announce about Christ" or "proclaim the truth about Christ," but it is
structurally impossible in a number of languages to "preach a person."
In such cases, this first sentence may be most aptly rendered as "and so
we tell everyone about Christ."

We warn and teach represent participles in Greek; the first verb is fairly rare in the NT (8 times in all); it means "to admonish," "to warn," usually implying an act or conduct which is being condemned (compare Acts 20.31, 1 Cor 4.14, 1 Thes 5.14, 2 Thes 3.15, and see the noun in Titus 3.10). Here there is no statement of what this might be, but probably refers to the warning in the Christian message about the consequences of rejecting it. "Teaching" probably refers to the moral and ethical principles of the gospel. Others, however, understand that the "warning" is against errors (on the part of the new Christians) and that the "teaching" is the advanced instruction.

Since warn and teach are in a sense negative and positive respectively, their being placed together in this short phrase may seem rather strange and even awkward. It may, therefore, be necessary to indicate something of the content of warn and teach. Thus one may translate "we warn them about what they should not do and teach them what they should do."

Three times the Greek has "every man" (RSV), in order to stress not only the universal nature of the gospel but also the equality of all believers, without any distinction or discrimination: "warning everyone and teaching everyone...in order that we might present everyone..."

With all possible wisdom qualifies the manner in which the activity is carried out. Some take "in all wisdom" to indicate the content of the teaching (as Mft Gpd Phps; see also Brc NEB); others, as TEV and RSV, as the way in which the apostle and his colleagues do their work. As Abbott says, the object of the verb "to teach" in the NT is always in the accusative, not a dative phrase with the preposition "in."[4] Wisdom here may be God-given (so TNT) as opposed to human wisdom, but the context does not require this.

Since with all possible wisdom probably qualifies the manner in which Paul sought to warn and teach everyone, it is possible to introduce wisdom as a part of a preliminary participial phrase, for example, "being as wise as possible" or "by using all the wise words possible."

In order to bring...into God's presence translates the Greek verb paristēmi (see 1.22). The verb may imply a legal setting, with reference to the Judgment Day; others see it as a cultic term, both here and in 1.22. In order to bring...into God's presence may simply be translated as "in order to cause to come before God."

As a mature individual translates the Greek adjective "perfect," "complete." In mystery cults it described the minority who had been initiated into the secrets and rituals of the religion; Paul here again emphasizes the universal nature of the gospel. Everyone is to be "perfect," not meaning sinless perfection, but spiritual development and maturity, that is, a full knowledge of God's will and a devotion to follow it. It appears elsewhere in Paul's letters in 1 Cor 2.6, 14.20, Phil 3.15, and Col 4.12 (compare also Eph 4.13).

A literal rendering of as a mature individual may mean nothing more than "as an adult," and this is, of course, not the meaning of the phrase in this context. Since the term "mature" may refer only to an age or height, it may be better to emphasize "completeness," for example, "as a complete person" or "as a person who is not lacking in anything," but one must

avoid an expression which suggests no lack of physical resources or pos-
sessions. Accordingly, one may wish to translate this phrase as "not
lacking in any understanding."

In union with Christ: see 1.2. NEB "a mature member of Christ's
body." In this context in union with Christ may be well translated as one
who is linked with Christ."

1.29   To get this done I toil and struggle, using the mighty
            strength which Christ supplies and which is at work in
            me.

Now Paul switches to the first person singular, as contrasted with
the plural in verse 28 (GeCL, however, understands the plural in verse
28 as epistolary and translates by first singular).

To get this done may be expressed as "in order to accomplish this
task" or "in order to cause all this to happen."

I toil and struggle: the first verb denotes hard work; the second
one, in Greek a participle modifying the main verb, indicates trouble or
pain or effort (both verbs used together also in 1 Tim 4.10): NEB "toiling
strenuously," JB "I struggle wearily on" (which sounds like a complaint).
This verb agōnizomai describes a fight (John 18.36) or, more often, an
athletic contest (1 Cor 9.25, 1 Tim 6.12, 2 Tim 4.7; see the cognate noun
in Heb 12.1). It is used here generally in the sense of "struggle" (Wey
overdoes it with "like an eager wrestler").

Since the two verbs toil and struggle primarily reinforce one
another, they may be quite satisfactorily rendered by a single verb with
an attributive, as in the case of the NEB "toiling strenuously." For
example, one may say "I work very hard indeed" or "I work as hard as I
can."

Using the mighty strength which Christ supplies and which is at work
represents the Greek "according to his energy which is powerfully working."
By the use of the noun energeia (only 8 times in the NT, in Eph, Phil,
Col, 2 Thes), the middle participle of the cognate verb (energeō), and the
prepositional phrase "in power," Paul emphasizes the greatness and might
of Christ's power at work in him. RSV "inspires" is ambiguous and could
be misunderstood.

The phrase mighty strength must not be translated in such a way as
to suggest physical strength. It may be more appropriate in some languages to say "using the great power that Christ supplies," or "...makes
possible," or "...has caused me to have." Rather than saying "using the
mighty strength," it may be better to say "I can do this because of the
great strength." On the other hand, it may be necessary to restructure
this statement rather extensively and to say "I can do all this because
Christ makes it possible for me" or "...makes me able to do it." In this
way the expression of power is closely related to the hard work or toil
mentioned in the first part of verse 29.

In some languages, it may be quite impossible to talk about "mighty
strength...at work in me." A person may use strength in working but certainly "strength" does not work. Which is at work in me may, therefore,
be expressed as "which shows up as I work" or "which is manifest in what
I do."

2.1   Let me tell you how hard I have worked for you and
         for the people in Laodicea and for all others who do
         not know me personally.

Let me tell you represents the Greek "I want you to know." Though
the expression let me tell you is a more idiomatic equivalent in English,
it may be quite inadequate as a basis for adaptation into another
language, since it might suggest "permit me to tell you" or "allow me to
tell you." Paul is obviously not asking for any permission; he is only
introducing his statement in a relatively polite way. In many languages,
a dynamic equivalent of the Greek is actually a closer literal rendering
such as "I wish to tell you" or "I wish for you to know."
     How hard I have worked translates "the great struggle," the cognate
noun of the verb "to struggle" in the preceding verse. Paul's hard work
has been for the benefit of the Christians in Colossae, Laodicea, and in
other places where he was not known personally. Since it appears that
Paul was not personally known by the Colossians and Laodiceans, it is
probable that "and all those" means and...all others (so Lightfoot,
Abbott, Moule; see JB). The words could be translated, "indeed, for all
who..."
     A literal rendering of I have worked for you and for the people of
Laodicea might suggest that he had engaged in physical labor as an
employee of the people in Laodicea. This is, of course, not what is intended. Therefore, it may be better to say "how hard I have worked in
order to help you and the people in Laodicea" or "...in order to be of
benefit to you and to the people in Laodicea." The phrase the people in
Laodicea must be expanded in some languages to read "the people who
dwell in Laodicea" or "the inhabitants of Laodicea." On the other hand,
Paul is referring specifically to believers in Laodicea, and therefore,
in order to avoid a misinterpretation of Paul having labored for all
those living in Laodicea, one may better translate "for the believers in
Laodicea."
     Laodicea (see also 4.13, 15-16) was about 17 kilometers west of
Colossae.
     All others who do not know me personally may be rendered in some
languages as "all others who have never seen me" or "all others whom I
have not visited."

2.2   I do this in order that they may be filled with courage
         and may be drawn together in love, and so have the full
         wealth of assurance which true understanding brings. In
         this way they will know God's secret, which is Christ
         himself.[c]

         [c]God's secret, which is Christ himself; some manuscripts
         have God's secret; others have the secret of God the
         Father of Christ; others have the secret of the God and
         Father, and of Christ.

I do this should refer to the hard work which Paul has engaged in so as to help the believers in Colossae and Laodicea as well as others. It should not be merely a reference to his desire to communicate to them how hard he has worked. In other words, one may begin verse 2 by saying "I worked this way in order that they may be filled with courage."

In some languages, there is a problem involved in the shift from second person to third person. In verse 1, for example, the reference is to you as well as the people in Laodicea and all others, but in verse 2 the reference is merely to they. In reality, of course, the Colossians are not eliminated by this use of the third person plural pronoun, but the abrupt shift might suggest this in some languages. Therefore, it may be appropriate to say "I do this in order that all may be filled with courage..." or possibly "...you and they may be filled with courage..." Similarly, one may translate the second sentence of verse 2 "in this way you and they will know."

Filled with courage translates the Greek verb traditionally represented by "to comfort" (see KJV). It means "to encourage," "cheer up," "strengthen." In most languages, it is impossible to speak of "being filled with courage." One may "become very courageous" or as in some languages "have a hard heart," as a figurative way of talking about courage. In other languages, courage may be expressed as "willingness to face danger" or "facing danger without moving."

Drawn together translates sumbibazō "to unite," "to knit together," used in 2.19 and Eph 4.16 of a body being held together by its joints and ligaments. The verb may also mean "to instruct," "to prove" (compare Acts 9.22, 1 Cor 2.16), and so Vg "instruct" here; but no modern translation takes it in this sense. The figurative expression be drawn together in love is difficult to render more or less literally. One can, however, almost always speak of "coming to love one another more and more" or "become better friends by loving one another."

And so have represents the Greek kai eis, indicating the purpose or result of the preceding clauses. And so, as an expression of result, may require some such translation as "all this results in" or "because of all this you have."

In the phrase the full wealth of assurance, or "complete certainty," the Greek for wealth is being used again metaphorically to denote the precious value of the noun it modifies; assurance translates a Greek noun used only in 3 other place (1 Thes 1.5, Heb 6.11, 10.22); the cognate verb is used in 4.12, and appears in 5 other places in the NT.

The full wealth of assurance may frequently be translated as "you may be completely sure," or perhaps better "you may have the great advantage of being completely sure," or "you may be completely sure and this is very valuable for you."

True understanding represents sunesis (see 1.9); they will know translates the noun epignōsis (see 1.9,10). Which true understanding brings indicates the means by which one can arrive at assurance. This may be expressed in some languages as "true understanding causes this assurance." In a number of instances, however, one cannot speak of "understanding" without indicating something of the content of such "understanding," and therefore, one may wish to translate "if you understand the truth, this causes assurance" or "by understanding the truth one is certain."

[45]

God's secret, which is Christ himself stands for the Greek "the
mystery (or secret) of God, Christ." This text suffered many alterations
and expansions, ending finally in the text translated by KJV as "the
mystery of God, and of the Father, and of Christ." Mft translates another
reading, "of God the Father of Christ," Wey and JB "the secret of God."
(For a discussion of the textual problem, see Metzger, The Text of the
New Testament, pages 236-238.) The Greek text may be understood in four
different ways: (1) "the mystery of God, that is, of Christ," in which
"Christ" is in apposition to "God," (2) "the mystery of the God of
Christ," but the absence of the definite article before "Christ" makes
this quite improbable, (3) "the mystery of God Christ" (or, "the divine
Christ"), for which there is no parallel in the NT, and (4) "the mystery
of God, which is Christ," in which "Christ" is in apposition to the whole
phrase "God's mystery." This last one is the meaning accepted by the vast
majority of modern commentators and translators. What is meant by "Christ
is the secret of God" is that Christ reveals God's truth, which before
has been hidden from mankind (as the next verse makes clear); see also
1.27.

If one accepts the interpretation most generally followed by biblical scholars in which Christ himself is God's secret, then one may translate the last sentence of verse 2 as "in this way they will learn about
what God has not made known previously, and this is Christ himself." The
relationship between the secret and Christ may, however, be inverted in
some languages, so that the translation reads "in this way they will
know about Christ himself and he is the one that God has kept from being
known previously."

2.3   He is the key that opens all the hidden treasures of
           God's wisdom and knowledge.

The verse begins with the prepositional phrase en hō, RSV "in
whom." But this can be translated as the neuter, "in which" (so JB), referring to the word secret (verse 2).

Inasmuch as the meaning of the verse is that Christ makes God's
secret known, TEV has He is the key that opens for the Greek "in whom
are hidden" (see RSV). The apostle's argument is that Christ is the revelation of God's purpose, and so implicit in the text is that the hidden treasures of God's wisdom and knowledge are now revealed in Christ.
But most translators have, simply, "hidden in Christ." Gpd has "are to
be found," Wey "are stored up, hidden from view," GeCL "in him is contained everything that mankind can ever know about God." The verse emphasizes (1) Christ's sufficiency, that is, all of God's wisdom and
knowledge are revealed by him; and (2) Christ's uniqueness, that is, in
him and nowhere else, are the treasures of divine wisdom and knowledge
to be found. So Phps "in him, and in him alone..."

It is most likely that "the wisdom and knowledge" are God's (so
Moule, see NEB), and not just in general.

It is frequently necessary in translating to eliminate certain
figurative expressions which cannot be carried over from one language to
another. In this instance, however, a non-figurative expression is translated by a figurative one, namely, the key that opens. Though this idiom

is quite acceptable in English, it would be difficult to translate literally into a number of other languages, especially since the treasure
in this instance is not a literal object but a truth about God as revealed through Jesus Christ. An equivalent expression in some languages
may be "he is the one who reveals the hidden treasures" or "...causes
to be known the hidden treasures." It may, however, be necessary to
characterize the wisdom and knowledge as being hidden treasures, but only
as a postposed qualification of the wisdom and knowledge, for what Christ
really reveals is God's wisdom and knowledge. Therefore, one may translate "he is the one who makes known God's wisdom and knowledge which is
like a treasure which has been hidden." By changing the metaphor hidden
treasures to a simile by the use of "like," one may often make clearer
what is the relationship between wisdom and knowledge and treasures.

2.4-5   4 I tell you, then, do not let anyone deceive you
               with false arguments, no matter how good they seem to
               be. 5 For even though I am absent in body, yet I am
               with you in spirit, and I am glad as I see the resolute
               firmness with which you stand together in your faith
               in Christ.

Paul concludes this section by stating the purpose of the exposition
about Christ and his work: it is that his readers remain faithful to the
gospel.
Since Paul was writing a letter to the people in Colossae rather
than talking to them, it may be necessary to introduce verse 4 as "I am
writing to you" or "the purpose of my writing to you is..."
Do not let anyone deceive you: the Greek hina is probably to be
understood as an imperative (Turner 102, Moule Idiom Book 145); most (RSV
NEB JB NAB NIV Brc Gpd Mft Phps TNT) take it as purpose or result. The
verb "to deceive" is used elsewhere only in James 1.22, and means "to
convince by false reasoning, to delude, mislead, lead astray." Deceive
should not be translated in such a way as to suggest mere "cheating." The
appropriate meaning is sometimes reflected in a translation such as "convince you by lies." In some instances, this type of deception may be
expressed figuratively as "lead you down the wrong path" or "cause you to
leave the right road."
False arguments, no matter how good they seem to be translates the
Greek work pithanologia, which appears only here in the NT. NIV has "fine
sounding argument," TNT "plausible arguments," Gpd JB NEB NAB "specious
arguments." False arguments may simply be translated in some languages as
"lies" or "arguments which are lies." No matter how good they seem to be
may be rendered as "even if they sound good" or "even if they sound like
they are true."
Paul's statement about being absent in body but present in spirit
(also 1 Cor 5.3) carries no spiritualistic overtones, as though his "spirit"
could leave his body and go to Colossae; it is simply a way of stating his
sense of close indentification with his Colossian fellow Christians, even
though he is not physically present with them. Since one must avoid any
translation of absent in body and with you in spirit which would suggest

migration of one's spirit from the body in order to be present some place else, it is possible to render the first part of verse 5 as "even though I am not there with you, I am still thinking about you constantly" or "even though I am not present with you, you may be sure it is as though I were present."

The resolute firmness with which you stand together represents two nouns; taxis is a military term, meaning "orderly ranks," "columns"; stereoma means "firmness," "solidity," and is also used in military context. So NEB "orderly array and firm front," TNT "well-disciplined... firm faith," Wey "good discipline...solid front."

Resolute firmness may sometimes be expressed more effectively by a negation "you do not move" or "you are not pushed away." The relationship between the resolute firmness and the way in which the believers stand together may be expressed as "you join tightly together and no one can separate you."

Your faith in Christ: although possible, it does not seem probable that here "faithfulness to Christ" is meant; GeCL, however, translates "how firmly and unshakeably you remain in your trust in Christ." Your faith in Christ may be rendered in this context as "in the way in which you trust Christ" or "...have confidence in Christ."

TEV	(2.6-15)	RSV

FULLNESS OF LIFE IN CHRIST

6 Since you have accepted Christ Jesus as Lord, live in union with him. 7 Keep your roots deep in him, build your lives on him, and become stronger in your faith, as you were taught. And be filled with thanksgiving.

8 See to it, then, that no one enslaves you by means of the worthless deceit of human wisdom, which comes from the teachings handed down by men and from the ruling spirits of the universe, and not from Christ. 9 For the full content of divine nature lives in Christ, in his humanity, 10 and you have been given full life in union with him. He is supreme over every spiritual ruler and authority.

11 In union with Christ you were circumcised, not with the circumcision that

6 As therefore you received Christ Jesus the Lord, so live in him, 7 rooted and built up in him and established in the faith, just as you were taught, abounding in thanksgiving.

8 See to it that no one makes a prey of you by philosophy and empty deceit, according to human tradition, according to the elemental spirits of the universe and not according to Christ. 9 For in him the whole fulness of deity dwells bodily, 10 and you have come to fulness of life in him, who is the head of all rule and authority. 11 In him also you were circumcised with a circumcision made without hands, by putting off the body of flesh in the circumcision of Christ; 12 and you were buried with him in baptism, in which you were also raised with him through faith in the working of God, who raised

is made by men, but with the circumcision made by Christ, which consists of being freed from the power of this sinful self. 12 For when you were baptized, you were buried with Christ, and in baptism you were also raised with Christ through your faith in the active power of God, who raised him from death. 13 You were at one time spiritually dead because of your sins and because you were Gentiles without the Law. But God has now brought you to life with Christ. God forgave us all our sins; 14 he canceled the unfavorable record of our debts with its binding rules and did away with it completely by nailing it to the cross. 15 And on that cross Christ freed himself from the power of the spiritual rulers and authorities;[d] he made a public spectacle of them by leading them as captives in his victory procession.

[d]Christ freed himself from the power of the spiritual rulers and authorities; or Christ stripped the spiritual rulers and authorities of their power.

him from the dead. 13 And you, who were dead in trespasses and the uncircumcision of your flesh, God made alive together with him, having forgiven us all our trespasses, 14 having canceled the bond which stood against us with its legal demands; this he set aside, nailing it to the cross. 15 He disarmed the principalities and powers and made a public example of them, triumphing over them in him.[d]

[d]Or in it (that is, the cross)

In this section, Paul develops the theme of Christ's effective work in redemption, as opposed to the false teaching of the Colossian heretics. He reminds his readers of their initial experience in which they had accepted Christ Jesus as Lord, and to its practical consequences (2.6-7). He warns them not to be misled by purely human teaching, which is opposed to the true teaching (2.8), and with hardly a break he continues expounding the nature of their Christian experience (2.9-15).

In typical Pauline style, this section contains a number of dependent expressions. It consists of one short section (verses 6-7), an injunction to "live in union with him," followed by a long sentence beginning at verse 8 and ending at verse 15, which has three main parts. The first one (verses 8-12) is a warning to the readers not to allow themselves to be seduced by human error (verse 8), (a) because of who Christ is (verse 9) and (b)

[49]

because of what their experience with him has been (verses 10-12): (i)
they had received full life, (ii) they had been circumcised, and (iii)
they had been raised to the life with him. The second part of the sentence
(verses 13-14) describes the condition of the Colossians before their
Christian experience (13a), followed by a statement of what God had done
for them (13b-14). The third part of the sentence (verse 15) is a statement of the victory achieved by Christ (or God) at the crucifixion.

The whole section is somewhat complex; the relation between the
various clauses and phrases is not always clear, and in some places there
are differences of opinion about the subject of the verbs.

2.6   Since you have accepted Christ Jesus as Lord, live
        in union with him.

Since marks the transition to a new section; it is to be understood
in the logical, not temporal, sense; "because," "in view of the fact that."
Accepted translates the verb paralambanō, which is often used with personal
objects in the sense of taking to oneself or along with oneself. It is
also the verb which means to receive teachings or instructions as part of
a "tradition" (the verb paradidōmi "to transmit" being the complement of
paralambanō "to receive"). The verb is often used in this sense in Paul's
Epistles (1 Cor 11.23; 15.1,3; Gal 1.9,12; Phil 4.9; 1 Thes 2.13; 4.1;
2 Thes 3.6). Only here in Paul's Epistles does the verb have a personal
object, and so some see here the meaning "accept the Christian message
about Christ Jesus" (A & G s.v. 2.b.y; Lightfoot, Abbott, Moule). Translators have not attempted to bring this out explicitly, except Brc: "the
tradition you have received" (is that of Jesus as Messiah and Lord);
compare TNT note on "receive." A translation that attempts this should say
something like, "Because you have received the Christian confession that
Jesus Christ is Lord,..."

A literal rendering of you have accepted Christ Jesus as Lord suggests
in some languages that Jesus Christ was not actually Lord, that is to say,
a person is accepted as something even though he is not that individual.
Therefore, it may be important to change the expression in verse 6 to
read something like "you have acknowledged Christ Jesus as your Lord,"
or "you have stated, Christ Jesus is my Lord," or "you have acknowledged
the fact that Christ Jesus is your Lord."

Christ Jesus as Lord: there is the widest possible diversity of
opinion over the precise meaning of the Greek phrase: (1) Jesus as Christ
and Lord (Moule, Brc NEB); (2) Christ Jesus the Lord (Lohse; RSV NAB Phps);
(3) Christ Jesus as Lord (Peake; TEV GeCL TNT NIV FrCL); (4) the Christ,
Jesus the Lord (Lightfoot, Abbott; Mft JB TOB); (5) the Christ, Jesus, as
(your) Lord (Gpd); (6) the Lord Jesus Christ (SpCL).

Live in union with him: for the verb see 1.10; for the prepositional
phrase see 1.2. It may be quite unusual in some languages to render live
as an imperative, since a word such as "live" may suggest mere existence,
and this is something which does not seem appropriate in an imperative
form. Furthermore, the meaning of live in this context relates to behavior
or the manner of life, and therefore, it may be preferable to translate
"conduct yourself as one who is linked to him" or "...who is in union with
him."

2.7   Keep your roots deep in him, build your lives on
      him, and become stronger in your faith, as you were
      taught. And be filled with thanksgiving.

The verse is built on four participles which modify the main verb
"live" (in verse 6). To imitate the Greek construction of the sentence
(verses 6-7) makes it intolerably long and difficult to follow; so it is
better to break it up, as TEV has done, and start a new sentence in verse
7. Since these participial constructions introduce essentially the means
by which one may live in union with Christ, it is possible to begin verse
7 by saying "you can do this by keeping your roots deep in him and by
building your lives..."

Paul uses two figurative expressions: (1) "to be rooted in" (only
here and Eph 3.17), the figure of a tree or plant; (2) "being built upon"
(compare 1 Cor 3.10,12,14; Eph 2.20; 1 Peter 2.5; Jude 20), the figure of
a building. Christ is the "soil" into which the roots sink and also the
"foundation" upon which the building stands.

The more or less unusual nature of these figurative expressions may
require in a number of languages the introduction of similes instead of
metaphors, for example, "you should have, as it were, your roots deep in
him, and you should build, as it were, your lives on him..." The introduction of an expression such as "as it were"will immediately alert the
reader to understand the expression in a figurative sense. If neither a
metaphor or a simile can be employed, it may be possible to render keep
your roots deep in him as "remain firmly united to him," and one may
render build your lives on him as "as you develop in your life you should
be more and more dependent on him" or "how you live should depend more
and more on what he tells you to do."

Become stronger: the verb bebaioō (be or make firm, strong) is used
by Paul elsewhere only in 1 Cor 1.6,8; 2 Cor 1.21, and emphasizes constancy,
firmness, solidity. In your faith does not refer to a body of doctrines
or belief, but to a living relationship with Jesus Christ as Lord. Some
(compare Lightfoot, Beare) take tē pistei as instrumental, "by means of
your faith" (so Phps NEBmg); JB has "held firm by the faith" (similarly
Brc).

Rather than saying become stronger in your faith, it may be more
appropriate to render this expression as "believe more and more firmly"
or "put your confidence in Christ all the more." The strength of confidence
may, in some instances, be expressed negatively as "become completely
unmovable in your confidence."

As you were taught: most take this to modify the three preceding
participles ("being rooted...being built upon...being firm"); some, however,
take it to modify only the immediately preceding one "becoming stronger
in the faith." Some join it to the noun "faith": "the faith that you were
taught" (JB NEB Brc), but this does not seem very likely. The teacher here
would be Epaphras (see 1.7). In order to relate as you were taught to the
three preceding imperatives, it may be possible to state "you were taught
all this," or "this is what you were taught," or "you were taught to do
just this."

[51]

Be filled with thanksgiving: a typical Pauline stress on joy or thanksgiving as the hallmark of genuine Christian faith (see 3.16-17).

Some good manuscripts have here "abounding en autē ("in it," feminine) in thanksgiving," which gives the meaning "abounding in the faith in thanksgiving" (so KJV); others have "abounding en autō (in him) in thanks-giving," which means "abounding in Christ in thanksgiving" (so Vg). The vast majority of commentators and translations prefer the text as in United Bible Societies' Greek New Testament.

Though in both Greek and Hebrew it is quite common to speak of being "filled" with a particular emotion or experience, this is a relatively rare figurative expression in many languages. The abundance of thanks-giving may, however, be expressed by saying "be very thankful indeed," or "express your thankfulness much," or "show very much how thankful you are."

2.8   See to it, then, that no one enslaves you by means of the worthless deceit of human wisdom, which comes from the teachings handed down by men and from the ruling spirits of the universe, and not from Christ.

A literal rendering of see to it may suggest a positive value. It may, therefore, be necessary to alert the reader as to something which should not happen by introducing verse 8 by "beware of" or "be sure not to let happen that."

Enslaves translates a verb found only here in the NT (sulagōgeō) which means to lead away into slavery, an unusually vivid expression (Moule). The Colossians had been rescued from the realm of darkness and had been transferred to the kingdom of Christ (1.13), and now they were in danger of being made slaves again. JB "traps you and deprives you of your freedom" is good. Enslaves involved essentially a causative relation-ship, and therefore, one may translate "that no one causes you to become slaves" or "...makes you slaves."

The worthless deceit of human wisdom represents "the philosophy and empty deceit" (compare RSV). It is improbable that Paul is here referring to two different things; it is likely that "empty deceit" characterizes "the philosophy" he is talking about (one definite article governs the whole phrase). The Greek word philosophia appears only here in the NT (see "philosophers" in Acts 17.18). Here it means what is merely human wisdom, as contrasted with the divine wisdom in the Christian message. The word for "deceit" appears also in Matt 13.22, Mark 4.19, Eph 4.22, 2 Thes 2.10, Heb 3.13, 2 Peter 2.13.

Various translations try, in different ways, to bring out the conno-tation of the phrase: Mft "theosophy which is specious make-believe," Phps "intellectualism or high-sounding nonsense," NIV "hollow and deceptive philosophy," Brc "arid and misleading intellectualism," NEB "hollow and delusive speculations," Beare "humbug masquerading as philosophy." For languages which do not have technical terms for philosophy and intellec-tualism, it may be appropriate to speak of "the kind of thinking that people do which is worthless and deceives." In this way all of the components

of the worthless deceit of human wisdom are introduced but grammatically
redistributed.

This kind of "philosophy" is characterized as coming from the
teachings handed down by men (TEV) or "human tradition" (RSV). In other
passages in the NT, wrong teachings are similarly characterized (compare
Matt 15.2,3,6; Mark 7.3,5,8,9,13; Gal 1.14; 1 Peter 1.18), in contrast
to the Christian tradition, which is of divine origin.

It is rare that one can translate literally teachings handed down
by men. An equivalent may be "the way in which generation after generation of people teach each other" or "the traditions which different generations teach to those who follow." Sometimes the reference to succeed-
ing generations is made quite specific by saying "what fathers teach
their sons" or "what grandfathers teach young men."

This "philosophy" is further characterized as coming from the
ruling spirits of the universe. There is much controversy over the meaning of this phrase (which appears also in verse 20, and Gal 4.3,9), ta
stoicheia tou kosmou. The noun stoicheion means, primarily, the basic
unit of which a series is composed, such as a letter of the alphabet, a
basic element of matter, a fundamental principle of doctrine. In Heb 5.
12, for example, it means (plural) "elementary teachings," in 2 Peter
3.10,12 it refers to the elements of matter (air, water, earth, and fire,
in Greek speculation). In general two possible meanings are seen here:
(1) "elementary teachings" either of a Jewish or pagan origin, with various beliefs and rituals (Lightfoot, Moule), which were in sharp contrast
to the Christian way of life; this is variously expressed in translations
(see SpCL NIV Brc; Phps "man's ideas of the nature of the world," Gpd
"material way of looking at things"). (2) Spiritual powers, "elemental
beings," of the same species as demons and evil spirits, which were
thought to rule the universe in general or the stars and planets in particular (Lohse, Beare; TNT Mft NAB NEB JB TOB). The majority of modern
commentaries and translations favor the "elemental forces" interpretation,
but it must be conceded (as Moule points out) that as yet no example of
the phrase with this meaning has been found in literature contemporary
with or earlier than the writings of the NT.

The interpretation of "elementary teachings about the universe"
may be expressed as "those ideas which people have about the universe"
or even "widespread concepts about the world." If, however, the second
interpretation is employed, then one may speak of "those spirits that
rule the universe" or "those powerful spirits in the universe."

And not from Christ is added for emphasis; whatever comes from
human tradition and from the cosmic powers cannot be from Christ.
(Whether or not Paul believed that the "ruling spirits" were real is of
no concern to the translator; in this passage he speaks of them as if
they were, and the translator must faithfully represent this.) The final
phrase and not from Christ is so far separated from human wisdom and is
so relatively elliptical that it may be necessary to employ a complete
clause, for example, "and this kind of wisdom does not come from Christ"
or "these deceitful ideas do not come from Christ." In a number of languages,
it is appropriate to employ a negative before the positive. Therefore, it may
be important to introduce not from Christ immediately after the worthless

deceit of human wisdom, for example, "this kind of wisdom does not come from Christ but from the traditions which one generation after another tells each other..."

2.9   For the full content of divine nature lives in Christ, in his humanity.

Beginning with this verse, and going through verse 15, in an extended meditation on Christ's nature, Paul shows why the Colossians must take care not to be swept away by wrong thinking.

The full content of divine nature: the word translated "divine nature" (or "deity" RSV) occurs only here in the NT. For the full content and lives see 1.19. As in 1.19, Paul here emphasizes that all of God's nature is present in Christ, not diluted or dispersed among intermediary spiritual beings. This does not imply, of course, that there was no more "divine nature" left in God, nor does it say that Christ is God. It emphasizes the reality of the incarnation, the uniqueness of Christ. The full content of divine nature may be expressed as "his being just like God" or "his being no different from what God is."

It is almost impossible in a number of languages to speak of a "divine nature living in Christ." One can readily say "Christ has this divine nature" or "Christ is just like God." To attempt a strictly literal translation would be to suggest in some languages that Christ possessed only some kind of divine spark of deity, but did not have the true nature of God.

In his humanity translates the Greek adverb sōmatikōs (only here in the NT, compare adjective sōmatikos Luke 3.22, 1 Tim 4.8), translated "bodily" by Mft RSV; Phps Brc NAB NIV "in bodily form," Gpd NEB "embodied," JB TNT "in his body," TC "incarnate," SpCL "in the person of Christ," FrCL "For everything that God is has become embodied in Christ, to be completely present in him." It does not seem that Paul means to say that the divine nature in Christ is a physical element (as "in bodily form" appears to indicate); rather he is stressing the reality of the divinity present in the human person of Christ. Lohse: the word indicates "that the divine indwelling is real" (compare Moule, Beare). (The idea that the "body" here is the church is held by a few interpreters; the majority, however, take it to be Christ's own body.)

In his humanity may be best expressed in some languages simply as "when he was alive on earth" or "when he lived on earth as a person."

2.10   and you have been given full life in union with him. He is supreme over every spiritual ruler and authority.

Have been given full life translates the perfect passive participle of the verb pleroō, which is the cognate of the abstract noun plērōma "fullness" in verse 9. It would be wrong to take this passage to mean that Christians are likewise filled with the divine nature, as Christ is; in union with him they have reached "fulfillment," that is, salvation, and all that it means. Again the concept of "fullness," which is so familiar in the NT but often so difficult to render, must be rather radically altered in order to communicate essentially the same meaning, for example, "you have really been given true life" or "God has caused you to truly live." Sometimes the concept of "fullness" may be introduced by a negation, for example, "there is nothing lacking in the way in which God has caused you to live."

In union with him may indicate the condition which exists when one has this new type of life, therefore, rendered as "when you are in union with him"; or it may suggest a means by which this full life is realized, "by being joined closely to him."

Christ is here described as supreme over every spiritual ruler and authority. The context clearly shows that these rulers and authorities are spiritual, not human (see 1.16). "Head" (RSV) is used metaphorically of Christ also in 1 Cor 11.3, Eph 1.22, 4.15, 5.23, Col 1.18. Supreme over may be expressed as "to be more important than" or somewhat better as "to rule over."

As in other instances, it may be important to translate spiritual as "spirit," and the nouns ruler and authority as verbs, for example, "over every spirit that rules and has authority."

2.11   In union with Christ you were circumcised, not with the circumcision that is made by men, but with the circumcision made by Christ, which consists of being freed from the power of this sinful self.

Paul compares the Christian experience with the Jewish rite of circumcision, which was the sign of the covenant that God had made with the people of Israel (Gen 17.9-14); the rite, which consisted in cutting off the foreskin of every male child one week after birth, marked the boy as a true Israelite, a member of the covenant community. Paul says that there is a "Christian circumcision," which is the common experience of all believers, as they are related by faith to Christ, as they are in union with Christ. In union with Christ may suggest not only the attendant circumstances but also the means, for example, "as you were united with Christ" or "by your being united with Christ."

For people who are perfectly familiar with circumcision, there is usually no problem involved in using a general term to designate this rite. In some circumstances, however, even though circumcision is well known by the people, the expression used to refer to it may be regarded as vulgar. Therefore, one cannot use the normal designation. However, it is sometimes possible to employ a descriptive phrase such as "cutting of the body" or "cutting of the skin." For those languages which have no term for circumcision, it is always possible to borrow a foreign term and to provide a descriptive explanation in a footnote or in a word list in the appendix. A somewhat better solution is a general descriptive expression which is sufficiently ambiguous as not to have vulgar connotations, for example, "a scar on the body" or "a marking in the skin." Such an expression may, of course, be misinterpreted as referring to a tribal symbol of scarification, but this would constitute a rather close parallel, in that circumcision identified a Jew as belonging to a religious and ethnic community in the same way that certain patterns of scars on the face or body of people, particularly in Africa, identify tribal member-ship.

This circumcision is not made by men, that is, is not of human origin (lit. "not made with hands"; compare Mark 14.58, "a temple," 2 Cor 5.1, "a house," Heb 9.11, "the tent"). It is the circumcision made by Christ (see Beare); the literal "the circumcision of Christ" (RSV) could be understood as the circumcision performed on Christ.

Not with the circumcision that is made by men may be rendered as "this is not the kind of circumcision that men cause" or "this is not the kind of cutting done by men" or "...by people."

The contrastive expression but with the circumcision made by Christ can be badly misinterpreted if translated literally, for it would appear as though Christ himself was the one who circumcised each believer. It may, therefore, be necessary to say "but this circumcision is the one caused by Christ" or "...produced because of Christ."

One of the principal difficulties involved in verse 11 is the fact that the particular type of circumcision being referred to is only described in the final clause. It may, therefore, be useful to place the final clause immediately after the first clause, that is to say, after in union with Christ you were circumcised.

This "Christian circumcision" is not a physical cutting off, but a spiritual one, defined as being freed from the power of this sinful self. The Jewish rite consisted of the removal of the foreskin; the Christian counterpart consists of the removal of "the body of flesh" (RSV), which is Paul's way of saying "sinful self," that is, the whole person, not merely the physical or the sensual, which is characterized as sinful (compare Beare). The noun translated "putting off" (RSV) occurs only here in the NT; compare the cognate verb in 2.15, and 3.9 ("put off the old self with its habits"). Beare: "the corrupt personality as a whole--what man is in himself apart from the regenerating grace of God." NIV is good; "the putting off of your sinful nature."

In describing the circumcision made by Christ as being "the putting off of the body of flesh," there is a kind of mixed metaphor involving a shift from "cutting" to "putting off (of clothing)." However, the idea of "shedding one's sinful self" may cause certain complications, since the sinful nature can scarcely be regarded as merely some kind of clothing. In some languages a similar term may be used. For example, a snake shedding its skin or a butterfly escaping from a pupa might seem far more appropriate and has been used, in some instances, with effectiveness. The shift in the TEV to being freed from the power of reflects a radical change in the metaphor. This concept can perhaps be expressed most effectively in some languages as "no longer being under the power of," or "no longer being controlled by," or even "no longer having the sinful self telling us what we must do."

In a number of languages, it is extremely difficult to talk about this sinful self, though in some instances there is a somewhat parallel expression such as "the little man that lives within me" or "my innermost being." More frequently, however, one must speak of some organ of the body as reflecting both desire and plan. In some languages one can say "no longer controlled by my heart which is sinful" or "...wishes to sin."

In other languages, however, it may be inappropriate to characterize the heart as being essentially sinful, since the heart is sometimes equivalent to the conscience. Accordingly, it may be better to use a somewhat more general term, for example, "that part of me which wants to sin" or "...do evil."

2.12   For when you were baptized, you were buried with Christ, and in baptism you were also raised with Christ through your faith in the active power of God, who raised him from death.

This verse explains what Paul means by "Christian circumcision": it is the spiritual transformation depicted in the Christian rite of baptism. The structure of the sentence in Greek clearly reveals his thinking: "[11] ...in union with him you were circumcised...[12]having been buried (or, because you were buried) with him in baptism."

The Greek word for baptism here is the active form baptismos (elsewhere the passive baptisma). It may be that the act of baptism is here being stressed, in contrast with the result of the act, denoted by the passive form (so Lightfoot). But it is highly improbable that any such subtle distinction occurs between this passage and Rom 6.4.

Whenever possible it is important to use a term for baptism which will be acceptable to all groups practicing this Christian rite. The tendency has been to use a transliterated borrowing based either on Greek or upon some modern language. In this way unnecessary controversy can usually be avoided. In some instances, a rather technical expression for baptism has arisen which is acceptable to all concerned. For example, in the Maya language of Yucatan, baptism is described as "to enter the water," a phrase first used by Roman Catholics, then by Presbyterians, and now by a number of different groups many of which practice immersion. In a number of areas, an expression such as "water ceremony" has been employed. In this way no specific mention is made of the quantity of the water nor the type of contact between the water and the baptized person. In some instances, a more specific expression such as "washing ceremony" has arisen and is generally accepted by most Christian groups to designate all the different types of baptism. In certain instances, immersionists have later reacted against such terminology, considering it incompatible with their practice. They have therefore insisted on having in their own translations or editions of the Scriptures a term meaning "to dip beneath the surface." It is unfortunate when differences with regard to relatively secondary matters tend to figure so largely in people's reaction to particular translations, and accordingly every effort should be made to employ a completely neutral expression.

You were buried with Christ: the verb sunthaptomai occurs elsewhere only in Rom 6.4, "by our baptism, then, we were buried with him." This "burial" took place as the person was lowered into the water, and the accompanying "resurrection," as he or she was being brought up out of the water. Baptism symbolized death and resurrection with Christ, the end of the old self and the beginning of a new life.

The statement you were buried with Christ must often be marked as a figurative expression by means of an expression such as "as it were" or "like," for example, "you were buried, as it were, with Christ" or "it is just like you had been buried with Christ." Only in this way is the reader likely to grasp the significance of this figurative usage in which baptism is spoken of as a kind of burial.

A literal rendering of buried with Christ might suggest "buried alongside of Christ," which is obviously not what the expression means. Accordingly, it may be necessary to translate "buried in the way Christ was buried."

The phrase in baptism must frequently be expanded into an entire clause, for example, "when you were baptized" or "at the time of your being baptized."

You were also raised with Christ: the only other occurrences of sunegeirō are in 3.1, Eph 2.6. This spiritual resurrection is effected through your faith in the active power of God. For "active power" see 1.29.

The passive expression you were also raised must in many languages be made active, and therefore one may say "God also raised you up" or "God gave you new life." It may also be necessary, in this context, to indicate that "being raised" is figurative. Obviously the person is not literally buried nor is he literally caused to live again. Therefore, one may wish to translate you were also raised as "you were also, so to speak, caused to live again." If God is made the subject of the raising from the dead, it would be important to translate as "God also caused you to live again by his power."

A literal rendering of with Christ might suggest that the baptized people were raised up at the precisely same time that Christ was raised from the dead. This would apply only to those who had been baptized before Christ's death. It may, therefore, be important to render with Christ as "even as Christ was raised." More often however one may use a somewhat expanded phrase which will not suggest immediate association, for example, "along with Christ."

In the series of phrases through your faith in the active power of God, both faith and the active power of God are connected with the resurrection. The active power of God is not only the goal of faith but it is also the instrument for the resurrection. The faith, may therefore be interpreted as an essential element in the resurrection but not necessarily the instrument of it. As an essential element in the process, it is often expressed as a type of secondary cause. As a result, the central section of verse 12 may be rendered as "when you were baptized, God caused you also to live again, as it were, by his power. He raised you up, as it were, along with Christ. This happened as a result of your confidence in God's power." Only in this way can one sometimes reflect satisfactorily a series of prepositional phrases such as with Christ, through your faith, in the active power, and of God.

Who raised him from death: literally "from dead ones," the idea being that of the world of dead people whose company a person joins at death. Who raised him from death may be translated as "who caused Christ to live again" or in some languages "who gave back to Christ his life."

2.1   You were at one time spiritually dead because of your

> sins and because you were Gentiles without the
> Law. But God has now brought you to life with
> Christ. God forgave us all our sins;

Continuing the thought of what baptism represents, Paul refers to the fact that his readers had been spiritually dead, clearly the meaning of the Greek "dead" (RSV). In some languages, it may be best to speak of "being dead" as a simile, for example, "being dead, as it were" or even "just like dead." More often, however, it is helpful to employ a qualifying expression, for example, "dead in your spirits." In certain instances one can also use "dead toward God" or "dead as far as God is concerned," with the meaning of dead in relationship to God.

This spiritual death had been caused (or was characterized) by two circumstances, says Paul: your sins and the fact that you were Gentiles without the Law. The Greek word for sins is one which stresses the willful act of disobeying God's law, but in translating this term for "sins," it is not necessary to look for an expression different from the one used in 1.14 (where another Greek word is used).

The phrase because of your sins can best be expressed in most languages as "because you customarily sinned." It is normally necessary to indicate either by the word chosen for "sin" or by means of some expression of aspect that it was a characteristic of the person to sin, not merely the fact of having committed a particular sin or series of sins.

Gentiles means literally "the uncircumcision of your flesh" (RSV). For the Jews the rite of circumcision was the sign that they were God's people, bound to him by the covenant and governed by the Law of Moses, obedience to which insured their continued status as the chosen people. Translations have handled this phrase in a number of ways: SpCL BrCL "you were uncircumcised," FrCL "you were uncircumcised, you were pagans," GeCL "you had sinned and had not yet been circumcised by Christ," (which could be misunderstood, if read out of context), TNT "because, as Gentiles, you had never been circumcised," Brc "uncircumcised strangers to God," NEB "morally uncircumcised." In order to render the term Gentiles, a number of translators have transliterated the expression, but this usually does not prove to be satisfactory. Some have employed a phrase such as "other peoples" or "the nations," but too often this is understood only in a local sense and refers only to people of different nearby languages or tribes. Increasingly, the most common way of rendering Gentiles is to talk about "non-Jews." This generally provides the best setting for a satisfactory understanding of the term. Any attempt to designate Gentiles as those who are "uncircumcised" may run into serious complications in a number of languages since the "uncircumcised" would by no means include all non-Jews, especially in those areas of the world where circumcision is rather widely practiced. The only way in which one might approximate the NEB "morally uncircumcised" would be to speak of "being, as it were, uncircumcised as far as your hearts are concerned," but such an expression would involve such a radically mixed metaphor as to result in considerable misunderstanding.

The phrase without the Law must often be expressed as a relative clause, for example, "who do not have the Law" and in this context, as well as in many others, it may be necessary to speak of "the Law of Moses" or "the Law given by God through Moses." It is important to avoid an expression which would specify law in general or traditional customs, since in this context the reference is to the Law of the OT.

Having referred to their previous condition with a participial clause (ontas), Paul now describes the central fact of their new life with the principal verb "he made (you) alive together (with him)." This verb (sunzoōpoieō) is found only here and Eph 2.5; the simple "to make alive" is used by Paul in Rom 8.11; 1 Cor 15.22,36,45; 2 Cor 3.6; Gal 3. 21 (also John 5.21; 6.63; 1 Peter 3.18). For a discussion of the basic problems involved in God has now brought you to life with Christ see the comments under verse 12 for the clause you were also raised with Christ.

God forgave is in Greek an aorist participial clause, stating either the means by which God makes them alive or what he did at the same time that he made them alive. This latter interpretation is Beare's view, who classifies it as "the aorist of coincidental action." The Greek verb for "forgive" (charizomai) is used also in 3.13. In the biblical sense, forgiveness has to do primarily with God's restoration of the relationship between himself and man which has been broken by man's sin. It does not mean, or imply, the suspension of sin's consequences, which are seen as divine punishment. Us here includes all Christians. Later Greek manuscripts have "you," a change made to agree with the preceding "you" (see KJV).

Some languages make a very clear distinction between sin as an active event and the guilt which results from such evil actions. What is forgiven is the actual guilt, and such a term may need to be added to words for forgive which mean literally "to wipe away," or "to rub out," or "to turn one's back on." For God does not wipe out the event, but he does eliminate the burden of guilt and thus restores man to fellowship with himself.

2.14   he canceled the unfavorable record of our debts
              with its binding rules and did away with it com-
              pletely by nailing it to the cross.

Paul compares the act of forgiveness of sins to the cancelation of a record of debts. The subject of the verbs (two participles, one before and one after the finite verb) in TEV and RSV continues to be God (from verse 13).

He canceled is the Greek verb for "wipe out, erase"; used also in Acts 3.19 (sins), Rev 3.5 (name), 7.17, 21.4 (tears); the corresponding Hebrew verb in the OT is often used also with "sin(s)" as the object (compare Psa 51.9, 109.14, Isa 43.25). In order to express the concept of canceled, it is possible in some languages to use a phrase such as "to tear up," "to throw away," or "to declare that it is no longer valid."

The...record of our debts represents a Greek noun which is literally "a handwritten document"--an IOU, (that is, "I owe you") personally signed by the debtor, acknowledging his debt. The...record of our debts may be rendered as "the paper that says how much we owe," or "the list of all that we owe," or "the page that tells how many are our debts."

Unfavorable translates two separate phrases; even RSV telescopes the two: "which stood against us" (compare KJV "the handwriting of the ordinances that was against us, which was contrary to us"). It is unnecessary to represent both in translation. In a number of instances, unfavorable can best be rendered simply as "how much we had to pay," or "debts against us," or as in some cases "debts against our name."

With its binding rules is simply the dative, without a preposition, and its relation to the preceding is uncertain. Perhaps "because" (so Lohse); and commentaries give other possibilities. Paul is saying that God not only forgave man's debts, but also did away completely with the legislation that made him a debtor. The "legislation" is the Mosaic Law, and some translations make this explicit: "the decrees of the law" (NEB Brc), "the law's demands" (TNT). With its binding rules may sometimes be translated as "with rules governing what we must do" or "with laws saying, You must not do that."

Did away with it completely is literally "removed it from the midst"; the verb is used with "sins" as object in John 1.29, 1 John 3.5. The pronoun it refers here to the record of our debts, but it may seem rather strange to speak of doing away with a record by "nailing it to the cross." The point is not that the record was destroyed in the process, but that it was made no longer valid in the sense that the death of Christ on the cross wiped out our indebtedness. Therefore, did away with it may be expressed as "made it ineffective," or "caused it to no longer have power," or even "destroyed its meaning."

Nailing it to the cross: by use of this figure Paul says that the forgiveness of sins was accomplished by the crucifixion of Christ (for similar expression see 1 Peter 2.24). Moule comments that there seems to be no evidence for the alleged custom of canceling a bond by piercing it with a nail.[5] Nor does the figure here seem to allude to the cancelation of a bond by marking it out with an X, that is, crossing it out. Nailing it to the cross may be expressed as "attaching the record to the cross with a nail" or "using a nail to put the record on the cross," but since this expression is essentially figurative, it may be necessary, as in other instances, to mark the figurative usage by means of an expression indicating similarity or likeness, for example, "nailing it, so to speak, to the cross" or "as it were, nailing it to the cross."

The matter of the subject(s) of the verbs in verses 13-15 should be considered. In Greek "God" is clearly the subject of the verb in verse 13 "he made you alive (with him)," and thereafter there is no name or pronoun to identify the subject of the remaining verbs. Most translations and commentaries take God as the subject of all the verbs in verses 13-15 (Peake, Abbott, Beare, Lohse; GeCL RSV FrCL JB NAB NEB TNT Mft NIV Brc TOB Gpd; Wey seems to make Christ the subject of all the verbs). Lightfoot, however, feels that there must be a change of subject somewhere, since in his understanding the first participle in verse 15 can hardly have God for a subject; consequently, he makes the change with the finite verb in verse 14, "he set aside" (RSV). Moule also makes a change of subject, but with the first participle "having canceled" (RSV) in verse 14; TEV SpCL BrCL make the change in verse 15, with Christ as the subject of the verbs.

The determining factor is the understanding of the first participle in verse 15, whether it refers to an action taken by God or whether it must be related to Christ.

2.15   And on that cross Christ freed himself from the power of the spiritual rulers and authorities;[d] he made a public spectacle of them by leading them as captives in his victory procession.

[d]Christ freed himself from the power of the spiritual rulers and authorities; or Christ stripped the spiritual rulers and authorities of their power.

Perhaps the best way to display the various ways in which this verse has been interpreted is to set them forth in a schematic arrangement, before considering the specific words. The subject of the verbs may be (A) God or (B) Christ. The participle apekdusamenos may be taken as (1) active or (2) middle. Its object (a) may be "rulers and authorities" or (b) it may have no object.
    A.1.a: "God disarmed the powers": Peake, Abbott, Lohse, Beare; RSV Gdp Phps NEBmg NAB NIV JB FrCL GeCL TOB.
    A.2.a: "God divested himself of the powers": TC NEB. (Mft has a variant on this: "God cut away the angelic Rulers and Powers from us.")
    B.1.a: "Christ disarmed the powers": TEVmg SpCL BrCL.
    B.2.a: "Christ freed himself from the powers": Lightfoot, Moule; TEV TNT.
    B.2.b: in this interpretation, the participle apekdusamenos is understood absolutely, and the accusative phrase "the rulers and authorities" is taken as the object of the following finite verb "he made an example of them." In this case the implied object of "Christ stripped away (from himself)" is "his body," an interpretation favored by the Latin Fathers (apud Lightfoot), and adopted by J.A.T. Robinson (The Body, page 41), and in NEBmg.
    And at the end of the verse the prepositional phrase en autō may be taken as meaning "in Christ" or "in the cross." Most take it to mean "in the cross," either with God as the subject of the preceding verbs (Abbott, Peake; RSVmg TC TNT JB NEB NIV Mft Brc TOB FrCL; and, by implication, Phps GeCL), or with Christ as the subject (Lightfoot, Moule; Wey TEV TNT SpCL BrCL). Some who take God as the subject take en autō to be "in Christ": Lohse, Beare; RSV Gpd NAB. Vg takes en autō to be reflexive (=en hautō), "in himself."
    Faced with such a bewildering variety of possibilities, the translator must decide which seems most probable, and provide alternative renderings in the margin, though it is by no means necessary to introduce all of the alternative possibilities.
    Freed himself (TEV) or "disarmed" (RSV): the verb apekduomai (only here and in 3.9; the cognate noun apekdusis only in 2.11) means "to strip off, divest, take off (like clothing)." If taken as a middle it means "he stripped himself"; if as an active, "he stripped the rulers and authorities." The form is middle, but many understand it to have an active force (see

[62]

B1-D, #316; A&G; Lohse, Beare).

If one follows the TEV interpretation freed himself, it is possible to say "caused himself to no longer be under the power of." If, however, one interprets the verb in an active sense, then one may say "he took away the power of the rulers and authorities" or "he caused the rulers and authorities to no longer have power."

Commentators are agreed that "the rulers and authorities" are spiritual, supernatural, powers--so TEV the spiritual rulers and authorities. As in other contexts, it may be useful to translate spiritual by "spirits" and then to reproduce rulers and authorities by verbs indicating activities, for example, "spirits that rule and govern."

Made a...spectacle of them translates the verb which appears only here and in Matt 1.19 (compare the noun deigma in Jude 7). Public (RSV TEV and others) can be understood as "boldly" (so Lightfoot, Abbott, Moule); the noun parrēsia usually means "confidence, boldness."

He made a public spectacle of them may be translated as "he caused everyone to see," or "he showed them off" to everyone," or "what happened to them he made very conspicuous," or "he caused them to walk along behind him, so that everyone would see."

Leading them as captives in his victory procession translates the Greek verb thriambeuō, found only here and in 2 Cor 2.14. It refers to the well-known triumphal procession of a victorious general, leading captive rulers in chains at his chariot wheels. Compare JB "paraded them in public, behind him in his triumphal procession," NEB "led them as captives in his triumphal procession."

By leading them as captives may be expressed as "by having them tied up and walking along behind him" or "by making them march behind him with hands tied."

In his victory procession may be expressed as "as he rides along showing that he has been vicorious" or "showing that he has conquered these powers" or "...these spirits." But in view of the figurative usage involved in this passage, again it may be necessary to mark the expression as a simile, for example, "as though marching in triumph."

TEV	(2.16-23)	RSV

16 So let no one make rules about what you eat or drink or about holy days or the New Moon Festival or the Sabbath. 17 All such things are only a shadow of things in the future; the reality is Christ. 18 Do not allow yourselves to be condemned by anyone who claims to be superior because of special visions and who insists on false humility and the worship of

16 Therefore let no one pass judgement on you in questions of food and drink or with regard to a festival or a new moon or a sabbath. 17 These are only a shadow of what is to come; but the substance belongs to Christ. 18 Let no one disqualify you, insisting on self-abasement and worship of angels, taking his stand on visions puffed up without out reason by his sensuous mind,

angels. For no reason at all, such a person is all puffed up by his human way of thinking 19 and has stopped holding on to Christ, who is the head of the body. Under Christ's control the whole body is nourished and held together by its joints and ligaments, and it grows as God wants it to grow.

DYING AND LIVING WITH CHRIST

20 You have died with Christ and are set free from the ruling spirits of the universe. Why, then, do you live as though you belonged to this world? Why do you obey such rules as 21 "Don't handle this," "Don't taste that," "Don't touch the other"? 22 All these refer to things which become useless once they are used; they are only man-made rules and teachings. 23 Of course such rules appear to be based on wisdom in their forced worship of angels, and false humility, and severe treatment of the body; but they have no real value in controlling physical passions.

19 and not holding fast to the Head, from whom the whole body, nourished and knit together through its joints and ligaments, grows with a growth that is from God.

20 If with Christ you died to the elemental spirits of the universe, why do you live as if you still belonged to the world? Why do you submit to regulations, 21 "Do not handle, Do not taste, Do not touch" 22 (referring to things which all perish as they are used), according to human precepts and doctrines? 23 These have indeed an appearance of wisdom in promoting rigor of devotion and self-abasement and severity to the body, but they are of no value in checking the indulgence of the flesh.[e]

[e]Or are of no value, serving only to indulge the flesh

It is difficult to decide how far this section goes. There is no doubt that in verse 16 there is a definite shift to a consideration of the practical consequences of what has preceded. Verses 16-19 hang together as a unit, and verse 20 begins "if you died with Christ," while 3.1 begins "if, then, you have been raised with Christ." Many make a break at verse 19 and begin the new section at verse 20 (compare United Bible Societies Greek New Testament, TEV FrCL TOB). But since verses 20-23 deal with the same subject (that is, freedom from rules) as do verses 16-20, it seems preferable to join them all together as one section (so Lohse, Abbott, Beare; GeCL Phps NIV NAB JB).

The section begins, "Therefore no one is to judge you..." (verses 16-17), and then "No one is to condemn you..." (verses 18-19), two parallel sentences which categorically refute the attempt by the false teachers to impose certain rules and regulations on the Colossian Christians. Paul denounces those teachers as having broken off any vital relationship to Christ and thus any relationship with his body, the Church. The Colossians

were in baptism united with Christ in his death, and so have been set
free from rules which are completely of human origin and have no real
value in controlling sinful impulses.

2.16   So let no one make rules about what you eat or
                drink or about holy days or the New Moon Festival
                or the Sabbath.

The verb krinō means primarily "to judge" (see, for example, in a
similar context, Rom 14.3). Here the more general make rules may be more
appropriate (compare GeCL "let no one dictate to you..."). Other ways of
translating it are "criticize" (SpCL Brc), "take you to task" (Mft NEB).
JB has "never let anyone else decide..." What you eat or drink: such a
regulation seems to be based on Jewish distinctions between ritually pure
and impure foods (see Rom 14.1-4, 1 Tim 4.3-5, Heb 9.10, 13.9; see also
Mark 7.17-20, Acts 10.10-16), or else springs from widespread Greek ideas
that by abstaining from food and drink (especially from meat and wine) a
person was able more adequately to worship the gods.
    Rather than distinguishing between solids and liquids, as we normally
do in Indo-european languages, a number of languages make a distinction
between "cold foods" and "hot foods," but this may have nothing to do with
temperature. Actually it is a classification which includes both solids
and liquids but is designed to embrace all kinds of foods, largely on the
basis of what is regarded as their effects upon the digestive and physiological processes of the body. Some translators have wanted to use such
a basic set of distinctions, but it probably is unwise since it introduces
a distinction which was not true of biblical times and which will cause
certain further complications in other passages. A more satisfactory
equivalent in such cases may be simply "foods that are chewed and foods
that are drunk."
    Other matters involved are holy days, the New Moon Festival, and the
Sabbath, which seem to represent yearly, monthly, and weekly cultic rites
(compare Gal 4.10; see 1 Chr 23.31, 2 Chr 31.3, Ezek 45.17, Hos 2.11). The
holy days are annual religious festivals; the New Moon Festival (only here
in the NT) was celebrated every new moon, and the Sabbath was the Jewish
weekly holy day, the seventh day of the week, a day for rest from physical
labor and for worship. Again this seems to point to a Jewish background,
but some commentators, like Lohse, see Greek influence here, since "the
elemental powers" (the ruling spirits of the universe, 2.8,20) controlled
the movements of the stars and thus determined the calendar of religious
rites and festivals.
    Holy days may be translated as "certain days each year when people
worship" or "those days which people each year set aside for worshiping
God." Sometimes holy days are simply "special days for worship."
    The New Moon Festival must often be expressed in the plural since
it refers to festivals which are celebrated each new moon. Sometimes
these are called "celebrations when the moon is thin" or idiomatically,
"celebrations when the moon is about to conceive," that is to say, in
anticipation of the waxing moon, regarded as a kind of pregnancy.
    The Sabbath must likewise be rendered in many languages as a plural,

for example, "those days each week when one worships" or "the weekly rest days." Since the Hebrew root underlying the word sabbath actually refers to resting, it is generally preferable to translate the Sabbath as "day of rest." It may then be appropriately interpreted by different groups as either the seventh day of the week or the first day of the week, though increasingly in various parts of the world, Sunday is being regarded as the last day of the week (a part of the "weekend"), and Monday is spoken of as the first day of the week. Accordingly, such phrases as "seventh day" and "first day" may involve complications because of shifts in meaning.

2.17   All such things are only a shadow of things in the
        future; the reality is Christ.

Paul characterizes these rules and the beliefs which they are based on as a mere shadow of things in the future, that is, they are unreal, they are not valid. What is meant by "what is to come" (RSV)? JB NEB TNT NIV translate "what was to come" (see Beare, Moule) which may better represent the idea, since the reality has already come in Christ. So the translation may be "They are only a shadow of things to come" or "They are only a shadow of what was to come." For a similar distinction between Jewish Law and the Gospel see Heb 8.5, 10.1.
The phrase all such things must often be translated as "such rules," or "such observances," or even "obeying such rules."
The concept of a shadow of things in the future may be extremely difficult to comprehend in some languages, for it may be difficult to imagine the future casting a shadow. In certain instances, however, one may speak of "a reflection" or even of "a mirror reflection." Therefore a shadow of things in the future may be expressed as "a mirror reflection of what will happen in the future." If, however, one assumes that the reference is to the past as something which has already occurred in the incarnation, then one may speak of "a reflection of what was to happen," and if necessary, as "a reflection of what was to happen and which did happen." Otherwise, the expression might be interpreted to mean that the purpose implied in such rules was actually voided.
The reality is Christ translates the Greek "but the body (is) of Christ." The word "body" is used occasionally in the sense of substance or reality, that is, what is real, true, as opposed to delusion or illusion (commentators cite passages in Philo and Josephus). Some commentators suggest that "body" here refers also and specifically to "the body of Christ," the Church, in which the real, as opposed to the unreal, has been made manifest. No translation, however, attempts to make this thought explicit (but see NAB "the reality is the body of Christ").
The reality is Christ may be expressed as "what is real is Christ" or "what exists is Christ."

2.18   Do not allow yourselves to be condemned by anyone who
        claims to be superior because of special visions and
        who insists on false humility and the worship of angels.
        For no reason at all, such a person is all puffed up by

his human way of thinking.

To be condemned translates the Greek katabrabeuō (compare brabeuō in 3.15, see brabeion, "prize," in 1 Cor 9.24, Phil 3.14), which appears only here in the NT. It means "to give an adverse decision" or "to deprive of the rightful prize," and is formed from brabeus, the judge or umpire at athletic contests. This expression has been handled in several ways: "disqualify you for the prize" (NIV), "rob you of your reward" (TNT), "cheat you out of your joy" (Phps), "do not allow yourselves to be deprived of victory" (TOB).

In view of the figurative meaning of the Greek katabrabeuō, one can readily see why and how a number of different English translations have employed quite different figures of speech, in contrast with the TEV which reads Do not allow yourselves to be condemned. One might also employ "do not permit anyone else to take away from you what is rightfully yours," or "...what really belongs to you," or "...what should be your reward."

The description that follows of these "umpires" is not easy to understand, and several interpretations are possible. It is expressed by three participial clauses, "insisting...taking his stand...being puffed up." The first clause is translated by RSV "insisting on self-abasement and worship of angels." The verb used here (thelō) ordinarily means "to wish," but here, with the preposition en "in," it is taken to be the Greek equivalent of a Hebrew expression meaning "to take pleasure in" (So Lohse, A&G 4b, Lightfoot, Moule; compare TNT NIV Brc FrCL TOB); others translate "of his own will" (Abbott, so Beare "as he wills," not as God wills); Gpd has "persisting," and RSV TEV NAB have "insist on."

There may be complications involved in a translation of who insists on, since this could mean "insists on for his own use" or "insists on other persons being involved in something." Since Paul is here condemning false teachers, it is important to indicate that these are individuals who "insist on others displaying false humility and worshiping angels."

The word "humility" is here used in a bad sense, that is, humility which is only superficial, not genuine; so TEV Phps NIV have false humility; some take the word as a technical term for "fasting" (Moule, Mft); TNT Brc have "asceticism" and NEB "self mortification."

The worship of angels: in this phrase angels are the object of worship. The worship of angels may be expressed as "bowing down before angels," or "praying to angels as though they were gods," or "treating angels as though they are gods."

Claims to be superior because of special visions translates a relative clause for which there are the most varied explanations possible. (Later manuscripts add the negative adverb; so KJV "intruding into those things which he hath not seen"). Commentaries should be consulted for possible meanings and suggested emendations of the text. Many base their interpretation on the use of the verb embateuō (see A&G for four meanings) in the mystery rites, which refers to entering the sanctuary after initiation, and so in this passage it describes those false teachers at Colossae as people who pride themselves on their superior status by virtue of the visions they had had. Lohse understands it to mean "as he has had visions of them (that is, the angels) during the mystery rites,"

Mft "presuming on his vision," TNT "insists on the importance of his visions," JB "are always going on about some visions they have had." Following this line of interpretation, it would seem that these false teachers were claiming superior status as the result of mystical visions in which they had apprehended reality, something which is denied to those who have not been similarly initiated into the cult.

Claims to be superior may be rendered as "says that he is better than other people," or "says that he is more important than others," or perhaps "says that he knows more than others."

In some languages, no distinction is made between dreams and visions, but in general there is a distinction between those particular visual forms which appear at night and those which come in the daytime or as the result of some particular ecstatic experience. Sometimes visions are spoken of as "dreams in the daytime." In other instances, they may be called "dreams which reveal" or "dreams which have truth." At any rate, one must avoid a term which simply suggests a nightmare.

Puffed up (see also 1 Cor 4.6,18,19; 5.2; 8.1; 13.4) is used metaphorically, "to puff up with pride," that is, "to be vain, conceited, proud." For no reason at all, such a person is all puffed up may be rendered as "such a person is all puffed up, but he has no reason for being so" or "...he cannot justify his being puffed up." In general, however, one cannot reproduce the figurative expression "puffed up," since this may very well be taken literally. However, one can often employ an equivalent type of idiom, for example, "they beat their breasts" (an expression often used in Africa to express pride and conceit), or "they pat themselves on the back," or even "they say they are great."

Human way of thinking is literally "the mind of his flesh." NEB has "worldly minds," NIV "unspiritual mind," Moule "his materialistic or sensuous outlook," Beare "a mind which lacks spiritual enlightenment." By his human way of thinking may be rendered as "because of the way he thinks just like all other people" or "because he is just like everyone else in the way in which he thinks." The unspiritual aspect of such thinking may be expressed in some languages as "because in his thinking he never thinks about God." In some instances, it may be important to indicate quite clearly the fact that the phrase by his human way of thinking is essentially an aspect of means, and this may be introduced sometimes as the subject of a verb of cause, for example, "his thinking just like all other people think causes him to be very proud, but there is no real reason at all for him being proud." This type of restructuring of relationships within the sentence may seem rather radical, and yet it expresses clearly the meaning of the underlying text.

2.19 and has stopped holding on to Christ, who is the head
    of the body. Under Christ's control the whole body is
    nourished and held together by its joints and ligaments,
    and it grows as God wants it to grow.

Has stopped holding on: this is how TEV has translated the participle, stressing the cessation of an action; other translations which make this explicit are NEB NIV TNT Brc. Has stopped holding on to Christ may be rendered as "no longer holds on to Christ," but the figurative expression "to hold on to" may be understood in some languages only in a strictly literal sense, and therefore, it may be necessary to express the meaning by some such phrase as "he is no longer loyal to Christ" or "ceases to depend on Christ."

For the head see 1.18; here TEV has made it explicit that Christ is the head. Because of the difficulties in the figure of speech involving body, it may be useful to make explicit again what body is being referred to. Therefore, one may say "who is the head of the body which is the church" or "who directs the church which is his body, and he is, as it were, the head." By introducing "head" by an expression which makes it a simile, the meaning may be a good deal clearer.

Under Christ's control represents the Greek "from whom" (RSV), which describes Christ as the source of the body's growth; in Greek "from whom" is masculine, the antecedent being "Christ," who is implicitly referred to by the feminine noun "the head." The phrase under Christ's control must sometimes be expressed as a clause, for example, "Christ guides the body" or "Christ controls the body."

Nourished and held together: the verb "to nourish" (see also 2 Cor 9.10, Gal 3.5, 2 Peter 1.5,11) refers to the food the body receives to make it grow. Held together is the same verb which in 2.2 is translated "drawn together." The emphasis is on the "communication of life and energy, and the preservation of unity and order" (Lightfoot). The body is completely dependent on the head, and if separated from the head, it cannot grow at all.

Joints and ligaments: as commentators point out, this is not an accurate scientific statement on how a body works, and must be understood as a popular view.

So much of this passage in Colossians is highly figurative, and therefore it is not at all strange if readers find difficulty in understanding the abundance of figurative expressions, many of which seem to be rather extreme. One can, in a sense, understand how the head is significant in nourishing the body since the food enters by means of the mouth, but it is not as easy to understand precisely the role of the joints and ligaments, and there is no explanation as to precisely what Paul has in mind. Furthermore, it may seem rather strange to speak of the body being held together by its joints, since the joints seem to mark divisions in the body rather than performing a unifying function. When there is no term in a language to identify all of the joints by some general term, it may be possible to simply speak of "at all those points in the body where different parts come together," or "at all those points in the body where the body bends," or "wherever in the body one can move."

Grows as God wants it to grow (literally "grows the growth of God") points to God as the one who ultimately determines the growth of the body, with Christ as the immediate source. Since Paul continues to speak of the church as the body with its joints and ligaments and growth, it is best to continue the figurative usage in the last clause, and therefore, one may say "and so the body grows just as God wants it to grow." If, however, the body has been identified as the church in the first part of verse 19, the meaning should be clear that this is not Christ's body or any particular body but a metaphorical body, namely, the church.

2.20-21   20 You have died with Christ and are set free
             from the ruling spirits of the universe. Why, then,
             do you live as though you belonged to this world?
             Why do you obey such rules as 21 "Don't handle this,"
             "Don't taste that," "Don't touch the other"?

Still combatting the rules which the false teachers at Colossae
were trying to impose on the Christians, Paul refers again to their death
with Christ, symbolized in baptism (verse 12a). The Greek is a conditional
clause, "if...you died" (RSV), which is a rhetorical device and does not
imply any doubt; it is a way of stating a fact, from which certain consequences are being drawn. Their "death" is a spiritual one, they have
died to the old life, which is controlled by sin (see further 3.3).

In place of the statement you have died with Christ, it may be more
relevant and accurate to translate "when Christ died, you also died." The
figurative meaning may, of course, be marked by some such additional phrase
as "as it were."

The expression are set free may be rendered as "are no longer under
the control of" or "have been rescued from."

For the ruling spirits of the universe see 2.8. In this context,
the ruling spirits of the universe may be readily rendered as "the spirits
that rule this universe" or "...this world."

You live as though you belonged to this world: although Paul does
not dwell on the idea in this letter, "the world" is dominated by the
power of evil and sin, from which a Christian has been set free.

The verb live in this context may be better expressed in some
languages as "conduct yourselves" or "behave as," for it refers not to
actual physiological life but to manner of behavior.

It may be quite easy to speak of the world belonging to people, but
very strange, if not unintelligible, to speak of "people belonging to the
world." In some instances, an equivalent expression may be "as though
you really were a part of this world" or "as though you were just like
everyone else in this world."

You obey such rules as translates the passive of the Greek verb
dogmatizō (only here in the NT, compare dogma in Acts 16.4, Col 2.14) "to
impose a rule"; the passive means "to submit to a rule, to obey a rule."
Such rules as may be better expressed in some languages as "the following
rules." In some languages, however, it is very important to make a
distinction between those verbs for "obey" which refer to obeying a person
and those which relate to conformance to particular rules. One may, for
example, "obey a person," but "live according to certain rules."

It is not entirely clear what is the specific content of the two
rules "do not handle...do not touch" (RSV). If a distinction is intended,
the first verb (haptomai) seems to be the stronger one, since it may be
used in the sense of having contact with, and even "possessing"; see its
use in 2 Cor 6.17, and 1 Cor 7.1 (which has "a woman" for object). From
its use in 1 Cor 7.1, some commentators see here some sort of regulation
which made sex taboo, but this does not seem very likely. It is more

likely that both verbs, together with don't taste, refer to certain foods
and drinks which the false teachers had proscribed (1 Tim 4.3 is explicit: certain foods and marriage were being prohibited).

The difficulty with the series of negations don't handle this,
don't taste that, don't touch the other is that frequently some kind of
concrete object is required. Indefinite pronominal forms such as "this,"
or "that," or "the other" simply do not suffice, and therefore one may
need to render these prohibitions as "don't handle this food; don't
taste that food; and don't even touch the other food." Such expressions
may be more helpful for the readers' understanding of precisely what is
involved, and by having nouns as objects, the grammatical requirements
are also fulfilled.

2.22   All these refer to things which become useless once
            they are used; they are only man-made rules and
            teachings.

All these refer: the regulations have to do with certain material
things, not otherwise specified, which cease to exist once they are used.
The language strongly supports the idea that food and drink are meant.
Become useless translates the phrase "into destruction"; they are
perishable and are meant by God to be used, to be consumed.

All these refer to things which become useless may require certain
modifications in order to communicate essentially the same meaning. For
example, all these must be translated somewhat more specifically in some
languages, for example, "all these regulations" or "all these statements
about what one must not do." The verb refer may be translated often as
"talk about" or "are concerned with." In translating things, one must
be careful to identify the right types of objects; for example, things
is too often translated simply as "artifacts," that is to say, things
that are manufactured. Here, however, the reference is primarily to food
and drink, and therefore, it may be necessary to simply say "about what
is eaten and drunk."

Which become useless must often be expressed as "which are no longer
of any value" or "which cannot be used again." The meaning is also re-
inforced by the final clause once they are used, and thus one may say
"which can only be used once" or "which are no longer of any value if
they have been used once." However, a literal translation of used may
likewise be misleading, since it might refer only to manufactured objects;
therefore, it may be more satisfactory to be slightly more specific about
the nature of the objects included in such regulations and therefore to
speak of "consumed" or even "eaten and drunk."

They are only man-made rules and teachings: this clause refers to
the "rules" in verse 20. The phrase is strongly reminiscent of Isa 29.13
(LXX), quoted in Matt 15.9. It characterizes the rules as being of purely
human origin, and not based on the gospel.

There is danger in a literal translation of they, since it may
refer to those things which become useless. It may, therefore, be better
to introduce a noun expression such as "these regulations" or "these
laws."

Man-made rules and teachings can often be best expressed as "rules which people make and what they teach."

2.23   Of course such rules appear to be based on wisdom
in their forced worship of angels, and false humility,
and severe treatment of the body; but they have no
real value in controlling physical passions.

Moule echoes other commentators when he says that this verse "is
by common consent regarded as hopelessly obscure--either owing to
corruption or because we have lost the clue."[6] He offers the following
translation: "which (rules about diet, etc.) have indeed a reputation
for wisdom, with their voluntary delight in religiousness and self-
mortification and severity of the body, but are of no value in combatting
sensual indulgence."
    The transitional emphatic phrase of course is equivalent in some
languages to an introductory expression such as "it is true that" or
"everyone knows that."
    Such rules may also require certain expansion, for example, "such
rules about what to eat and drink" or "statements about what you can or
cannot eat or drink."
    Appear to be based on wisdom (TEV) or "have...an appearance of
wisdom" (RSV) expresses the meaning most commentators and translators
attach to the rather unusual Greek phrase. Lohse translates "have the
reputation of wisdom." It may be particularly difficult to render more
or less literally an expression such as appear to be based on wisdom, for
this is semantically a very complex construction. Appear may be equivalent
to "many people think" or "many people are caused to think." To be based
may be rendered as "are justified by" or "are true because of." Wisdom
cannot be expressed, in many instances, as an abstract but must be
related to people who have the quality of being wise. Therefore, it may
actually be necessary, in some instances, to translate appear to be based
on wisdom as "people think that those who have made such rules are wise,
but they are not" or "people who have made such regulations seem to be
wise while they really are not."
    The three specific matters that appear to be based on wisdom are:
(1) "rigor of devotion" (RSV) represents a Greek word which appears only
here in the NT and which is translated as "self-imposed worship" or
"devotions" or "rigoristic piety" or the like. FrCL has "their worship
which springs from human will." Some commentators see this as a reference
back to "the (forced) worship of angels" in 2.18, and that is how TEV has
translated it; compare GeCL "self-chosen worship of the unseen powers."
(2) False humility is the same word as in verse 18 and has here the same
meaning as there. (3) Severe treatment of the body refers to asceticism,
the denial of normal bodily needs; it translates a word found nowhere
else in the NT.
    Their forced worship of angels may be rendered as "the way in which
they insist that people must worship angels" or, as expressed in direct
discourse, "the way in which they command,'You must worship angels.'"
    False humility may be expressed as "saying that they are humble
when they are not" or "pretending to be humble" or, as expressed negatively

in some languages, "saying that they are not at all proud."

Severe treatment of the body may be expressed as "not giving the body what it really needs" or "not supplying one's self with what is necessary in order to live." In some instances, a somewhat figurative expression may be employed, for example, "torturing one's body as a part of one's religion" or "saying that one can serve God by making one's body suffer."

The last part of the verse may be understood in two different ways: (1) these rules are of no value in controlling physical passions (so TEV RSV NEB NIV TNT Brc Wey FrCL SpCL BrCL); or (2) these rules are of no value at all: rather they only serve to satisfy physical passions (RSVmg, Abbott, Beare, Lohse, NAB TOB Gpd Mft Phps). Lohse sees two elements in the Greek and translates: "These things...have nothing to do with honor and only serve to satiate the flesh." GeCL represents another idea: "Actually these men search only for their own honor, and they satisfy their vanity." Before such a bewildering variety of possibilities, the translator must determine which one seems in better accord with the whole context of the passage and the letter. Dogmatic certainty, however, is impossible.

In rendering the interpretation of the TEV they have no real value in controlling physical passions, one may say "these rules do not help a person who wishes to control what his body wants" or "...the desires he has because of his body." If one adopts the second principal interpretation, one may translate "these rules about what one must or must not do, do not help even a little bit; they only satisfy what our bodies really want anyway." In some instances, "satisfy" may be expressed as "cause us to do."

With 3.1 a definite shift takes place from exposition to exhortation. Although there has been some exhortation in 1.3--2.23, and although there will be some exposition in 3.1--4.1, the two sections are clearly distinct in content and tone.

	TEV	(3.1-4)	RSV

3 You have been raised to life with Christ, so set your hearts on the things that are in heaven, where Christ sits on his throne at the right side of God. 2 Keep your minds fixed on things there, not on things here on earth. 3 For you have died, and your life is hidden with Christ in God. 4 Your real life is Christ and when he appears, then you too will appear with him and share his glory!

3 If then you have been raised with Christ, seek the things that are above, where Christ is, seated at the right hand of God. 2 Set your minds on things that are above, not on things that are on earth. 3 For you have died, and your life is hid with Christ in God. 4 When Christ who is our life appears, then you also will appear with him in glory.

These four verses establish the basis for the whole section and

contain the fundamental exhortation. Considering the fact that the
Colossians had died and had been raised with Christ, they are to aim
for the true values which are to be found in the realm of the glorified
Christ, who shares in God's glory. The meaning of their life is hidden
with Christ, and at his glorious coming it will be revealed as they
share in his glory. This is what it means to be "in (union with) Christ":
it is to share his death, burial, and resurrection, his glorious position
at God's right side, and his final coming in power. Thus the Colossians'
spiritual life and destiny are determined by the whole of Christ's
activity.

3.1-2   1 You have been raised to life with Christ, so
           set your hearts on the things that are in heaven,
           where Christ sits on his throne at the right side of God.
           2 Keep your minds fixed on things there, not on things
           here on earth.

With you have been raised to life with Christ (see 2.12) Paul begins
a new series of "with Christ" expressions, stressing the complete
identification of the believers with their Lord; in dying, their life
"is hidden with Christ," and at his coming they "will appear with him."
As in 2.20 the affirmation that they have been raised to life with Christ
is formulated as a condition (see RSV), but there is no doubt in Paul's
mind that they have, in fact, been raised. The form of the conditional
clause in Greek (ei) implies that the condition has been fulfilled. In
translating the first part of verse 1, it is almost always better to
use a statement of fact rather than a conditional clause, since a
condition can be so readily misinterpreted as something hypothetical
rather than real.
    You have been raised to life may be rendered as "you have been
caused to live again," but there may be serious complications involved
in the phrase with Christ, for a literal translation of life with Christ
might suggest "living with Christ" or "having one's life in union with
Christ." In this context, however, the emphasis seems to be that in the
raising of Christ from the dead, the Christian is symbolically himself
given new life. Therefore, it may be necessary in some languages to
translate "when Christ was raised from death, you likewise were, so to
speak, raised from death" or "...caused to have new life." In other
instances, the phrase with Christ may perhaps be best expressed as a
kind of means, for example, "by God raising Christ to life, he in a
sense also raised you to life."
    The connective particle so is particularly important in this context
and may require some expansion, for example, "and therefore," "and as a
result of this."
    Set your hearts translates the Greek "seek" (RSV), which is further
expanded in verse 2 by keep your minds fixed. No hard and fast distinction
is intended: desires and thoughts, wishing and thinking, the whole of
the emotional and intellectual energy is to be directed toward the above,
that is, heaven, where Christ reigns at God's right side. It is evident
that Paul is not advocating an attitude of utter disregard for everyday

responsibilities and duties which are laid upon believers; he is saying that their ultimate concern is with heavenly realities and values, determined by the presence and power of the risen Christ, who shares in the sovereign power of God.

Set your hearts on the things that are in heaven may be rendered as "desire what is in heaven" or "desire what God has for you in heaven." Again it may be necessary to avoid a translation of things which would suggest only material objects.

In many languages, throne may be rendered as "chair of authority" or "place from which judgement takes place."

Normally the expression at the right side of God is interpreted correctly, that is to say, on the favored side or the side of honor. However, in some parts of the world the right side is not the favored side but suggests demotion. It may, therefore, be important to translate at the right side of God as "on the honored side of God" or "in an honored position beside God." Some translators have thought that it might be useful to change completely the figurative language with regard to his throne at the right side of God, but such expressions are so frequent in the Scriptures that their complete loss or substitution by non-figurative expressions would probably result in a considerable measure of distortion.

Keep your minds fixed on things there may be rendered as "keep thinking about those things there." It may even be useful to combine the concepts of both thought and desire by saying "think about and desire what is there" or "...what is in heaven." By introducing "heaven," one may then mark even more clearly the contrast between "what is in heaven and not what is here on earth." In rendering things, it is important to have the focus upon experiences rather than upon objects.

3.3   For you have died, and your life is hidden with Christ
             in God.

So Paul states the reason why the thought and affection of the Colossians should be directed toward heaven. They have died (see 2.20), as their baptism testifies (see 2.12), and their life has been hidden with Christ in God. It is not easy to understand Paul's statement, except that it reflects the concept that the revelation of the complete meaning of a Christian's life must await the full revelation of Christ (verse 4); until then it is "hidden," just as Christ's real power and glory are as yet invisible. In God in Paul's letters is found only in 1 Thes 1.1, 2 Thes 1.1; the thought is that the believer's true life, his risen life, is identified with Christ's present unseen existence in union with God.

You have died must of course be understood in a figurative sense, and therefore it may be necessary to provide a clue to such an interpretation by saying "you have died, as it were" or "it is just as though you had died."

The clause your life is hidden with Christ in God is perhaps one of the most difficult expressions to communicate effectively in some languages. Your life is obviously more than mere existence; in fact the focus is upon the true life of the believer which will be revealed when Christ appears. But how to say that this true life is hidden in God and

[75]

together with Christ is extremely difficult. It may be best to interpret is hidden as "has not yet been revealed," since this would appear to be in line with the explanation of this meaning as it occurs in verse 4. With Christ can be interpreted as "as in the case of Christ," and in a sense in God actually marks the agent who has caused the life of the believer to be as yet unrevealed. On the other hand, it is also possible to understand in God as "by being closely related to God" or "in your relationship to God." Your life is hidden with Christ in God may, therefore, be rendered in some instances as "your real life is as yet not revealed, as also in the case of Christ, and all of this is true in view of your relationship to God" or "...because of your close union with God."

3.4   Your real life is Christ, and when he appears, then
        you too will appear with him and share his glory!

   Many good early manuscripts have your (TEV); others have "our" (RSV). If "our" is preferred, it is not to be translated as though it excluded the Colossians for it refers to all Christians. The statement "Christ is your life" is to be taken in its broadest sense possible; the real source, meaning, purpose, and destiny of the Christian's life can be defined only in terms of his relation with Christ (compare Phil 1.21). It is seldom possible, however, to translate your real life is Christ in such a way as to introduce all of the implications of this highly inclusive statement. In many instances, therefore, it may be necessary to be somewhat more specific, for one cannot simply identify life and Christ. In some cases one may perhaps best translate your real life is Christ as "your real life is to serve Christ" or "to serve Christ is really to live." In some instances, a condition may be introduced as a way of making the statement more generally applicable, for example, "if you really are to live, then you must serve Christ." A rather radical but justifiable restructuring of this statement may be found in the rendering "Christ alone can cause your life to have real meaning."
   When he appears, then you too will appear with him: this refers to the eschatological manifestation of Christ in power and glory, in which believers will participate (see 1 John 3.2 for the closest verbal parellel to this statement; and see 1 Peter 5.4, 1 John 2.28 for the use of the same verb phaneroō in connection with the final revelation of Christ). Share his glory represents "in glory" (RSV); Christ's glory here is his final revelation as Lord of all mankind.
   When he appears must be made slightly more specific in some languages as "when Christ appears on earth" or even "when Christ shows himself here again." In some languages, the addition of "again" is required in order to avoid the implication that the reference is only to the incarnation.
   Then you too will appear with him may be misinterpreted if rendered literally for it might suggest "coming again" or "showing up out of darkness." A closer equivalent in many instances is "then you too will be there with him."
   The exhortation to the Colossians to apply Christian principles in their lives follows as a consequence of their having been raised to a new life with Christ. What has happened to them must show its effects in what they are and what they do.

TEV   (3.5-17)   RSV

THE OLD LIFE AND THE NEW

5 You must put to death, then, the earthly desires at work in you, such as sexual immorality, indecency, lust, evil passions, and greed (for greed is a form of idolatry). 6 Because of such things God's anger will come upon those who do not obey him.[e] At one time you yourselves used to live according to such desires, when your life was dominated by them.

8 But now you must get rid of all these things: anger, passion, and hateful feelings. No insults or obscene talk must ever come from your lips. 9 Do not lie to one another, for you have put off the old self with its habits 10 and have put on the new self. This is the new being which God, its Creator, is constantly renewing in his own image, in order to bring you to a full knowledge of himself. 11 As a result, there is no longer any distinction between Gentiles and Jews, circumcised and uncircumcised, barbarians, savages, slaves, and free men, but Christ is all, Christ is in all.

12 You are the people of God; he loved you and chose you for his own. So then, you must clothe yourselves with compassion, kindness, humility, gentleness, and patience. 13 Be tolerant with one another and forgive one another whenever any of you has a complaint against someone else. You must forgive one another just as the Lord has forgiven you. 14 And to all these qualities add love, which binds all things together

5 Put to death therefore what is earthly in you: immorality, impurity, passion, evil desire, and covetousness, which is idolatry. 6 On account of these the wrath of God is coming.[f] 7 In these you once walked, when you lived in them. 8 But now put them all away: anger, wrath, malice, slander, and foul talk from your mouth. 9 Do not lie to one another, seeing that you have put off the old nature, with its practices 10 and have put on the new nature, which is being renewed in knowledge after the image of its creator. 11 Here there cannot be Greek and Jew, circumcised and uncircumcised, barbarian, Scythian, slave, free man, but Christ is all, and in all.

12 Put on then, as God's chosen ones, holy and beloved compassion, kindness, lowliness, meekness, and patience, 13 forbearing one another and, if one has a complaint against another, forgiving each other; as the Lord has forgiven you, so you also must forgive. 14 And above all these put on love, which binds everything together in perfect harmony. 15 And let the peace of Christ rule in your hearts, to which indeed you were called in the one body. And be thankful. 16 Let the word of Christ dwell in you richly, as you teach and admonish one another in all wisdom, and as you sing psalms, and hymns and spiritual songs with thankfulness in your hearts to God. 17 And whatever you do, in word or deed, do everything in the name of the Lord Jesus, giving thanks to God the Father through him.

[f]Other ancient authorities add upon the sons of disobedience

in perfect unity. 15 The peace
that Christ gives is to guide
you in the decisions you make;
for it is to this peace that
God has called you together in
the one body. And be thankful.
16 Christ's message in all its
richness must live in your hearts.
Teach and instruct one another
with all wisdom. Sing psalms,
hymns, and sacred songs; sing
to God with thanksgiving in your
hearts. 17 Everything you do or
say, then, should be done in the
name of the Lord Jesus as you
give thanks through him to God
the Father.

eSome manuscripts do not have upon
those who do not obey him.

The section is nicely balanced, with a succession of aorist imperatives tying the whole together through verse 14: "Put to death"
(verses 5-7), "get rid of" (verses 8-11), "put on" (verses 12-14). The
first two refer to habits the readers are to abandon, while the last one
refers to virtues they are to cultivate. The various units are not, however, artificially constructed. The first one (verses 5-7) lists five
sins which the Colossians are to put to death; the second one (verses
8-11) lists five more sins which they are to get rid of (verse 8),
followed by the command not to lie to one another (verse 9a), which is
buttressed by an eloquent statement of the reason of this command (verses
9b-11). The third unit (verses 12-14) lists five virtues which they are
to put on (verse 12), followed by the command to forgive one another
(verse 13). And to make the list complete, Paul adds the greatest of all
virtues, love, which holds all virtues together in a harmonious whole
(verse 14). Verses 15 and 16 read like addenda: "the peace of Christ is
to rule in your hearts" and "the word of Christ is to live in your hearts."
In verse 17 the summary comes, with the verb "you are to do (everything)"
unexpressed, but clearly implicit.

3.5   You must put to death, then, the earthly desires
                at work in you, such as sexual immorality, indecency,
                lust, evil passions, and greed (for greed is a form
                of idolatry).

For similar lists of vices see 1 Cor 6.9-10, Gal 5.19-21, Eph 5.1-5,
1 Peter 2.1, 4.1-3. Put to death: this verb occurs twice again (Rom 4.19,
Heb 11.12) in a literal sense; only here is it used figuratively (compare
the synonymous thanatoō in Rom 8.13), meaning "destroy, do away with completely"

(see also Rom 6.11). As Moule points out, the English verb "mortify" (as
in KJV), though etymologically accurate, carries today a different meaning
from what is commanded here.[7]

The figurative expression put to death is a forceful one and should
be retained if possible. However, it may lead to misunderstanding, since
"to kill desires" might suggest a complete loss of a desire to live. A
more satisfactory equivalent in some languages is "get rid of completely,"
or "eliminate completely from yourselves," or "cause completely to have
no more influence."

The earthly desires at work in you represents what is literally "the
members that are upon the earth" (compare KJV). It is an odd phrase, for
which no exact parallel has been found (see Rom 6.13). Lightfoot's explanation may be the best one: "the old man (see verse 9) with all his
members must be pitilessly slain," and he refers to Matt 5.29-30 for
similar language.[8] GeCL has: "therefore put to death what of the old man
still lives in you." Brc translates, "You must put an end to the use of
any part of your body for worldly and immoral purposes."

In a number of languages, there are two quite distinct words for
desires; one refers to appropriate desires and another to evil ones. It
is obviously the second term which is meant in this context, since all of
the specific designations for these desires are related to certain kinds
of sin. If a term for desires does suggest wrong desires, then it may not
be necessary to add a term for earthly. In fact it is rarely possible to
use an equivalent of earthly which has any reference to the earth itself.
The only way in which "the earth" can be introduced is in a rather elaborate
clause, for example, "desires which people in the world have."

It is rare that one can speak of "desires at work," for the very
fact that one "desires something" indicates that in a sense the desire is
active. Accordingly, the earthly desires at work in you, such as sexual
immorality... may be expressed as "your evil desires for unlawful sex..."

The first sin listed covers "every kind of unlawful sexual inter-
course" (A&G); indecency (TEV) or "impurity" (RSV) is usually associated
with sexual sins, and is joined to sexual immorality in Rom 1.24, 2 Cor
12.21, Gal 5.19, Eph 5.3, 1 Thes 4.7. The next word lust (TEV) or "passion"
(RSV) also refers to sexual passion (see Rom 1.26, 1 Thes 4.5), which
results in sexual sin.

In a number of languages, it may be difficult to distinguish properly
between indecency, sexual immorality and lust. Since all of these refer
to certain aspects of sexual sin, it may be possible simply to use an
expression such as "desire to engage in all kinds of unlawful sexual sins."
In some languages, an equivalent of these three expressions in Greek would
be expressed in figurative language, for example, "desires to act like a
dog," or "desires to be constantly hot with sex," or "constantly desiring
to rub bellies."

Evil passions (TEV) or "evil desire" (RSV) may be narrowly restricted
to sex or more broadly associated with evil of self-centered desire,
which is the basic cause of all sins. The noun itself may be morally
neutral or even good, and so the qualifying adjective "evil" is added.
If evil passions are to be interpreted in terms of sex relations, the
meaning may be incorporated or joined with the preceding three expressions.

If, however, evil passions are to be understood in a more general sense, the phrase may be translated as "desires to do evil" or "constantly wanting to do what is bad."

The Greek word for greed is literally "a desire to have more." In Eph 5.5 it is also made equivalent to idolatry. The reasoning seems to be that Mammon becomes the god that a covetous person worships and serves in the place of God (Matt 6.24). Greed may be rendered as "a desire to have many things" or even "a desire to have much more than others."

3.6   Because of such things God's anger will come upon
          those who do not obey him.[e]

          [e]Some manuscripts do not have upon those who do not
          obey him.

Because of such things must be rendered in some languages as "because people have such desires" or "because people desire to do such evil."

God's anger is the expression of the reason why God punishes sin and evil. On the part of some scholars (notably C.H. Dodd, in his commentary on Romans), there is a reluctance to use the word "anger" (or "wrath") of God because of its connotations; they would prefer to use something like "disaster from God" (so Moule); NEB has here "God's dreadful judgement," GeCL "God's judgement," SpCL "God's terrible punishment." It would be out of keeping with biblical thought, however, to think of this as the mechanical operation of a disembodied principle. What happens is caused by God, and such things happen because God is angry, that is, he is affected. He is not distant and unmoved by human sin, but expresses his anger by punishing sinners.

In translating anger, it is important to avoid the implications of "fury" or "hatred." God's anger is not an irrational, emotional reaction but a justified response to man's willful disobedience and sin. In an attempt to avoid the meaning of unreasonable fury, there is also the danger of introducing a meaning which is essentially equivalent to "being irritable" or simply being irritated because of man's sin. Such an expression seriously distorts the significance of the context. An additional problem is posed by the English expression God's anger will come upon those, for it is rare that one may speak of "anger coming." In general one must say "God will be angry with those."

Will come (TEV) or "is coming" (RSV): the present tense of the Greek verb either expresses a certainty and an immediacy which are better represented by "is coming" or "comes," or else is a conventional way of speaking of the Day of Judgement, in which case "will come" is more suitable.

Upon those who do not obey him: the phrase seems to have been added here from the parallel Eph 5.6; but a majority of the Committee that prepared the UBS Greek NT judged it to be original, and so included it in the text, though within brackets and graded as a D passage (see Metzger Textual Commentary, 624-625). Many modern translations omit it (RSV NEB JB NAB Brc NIV TOB); among those that include it are TEV FrCL GeCL BrCL TNT BJ. The phrase "the sons of disobedience" (RSV) is a Semitic way of talking about disobedient people, that is, people who disobey God.

3.7   At one time you yourselves used to live according
       to such desires, when your life was dominated by
       them.

The phrase at one time must not be interpreted as reference to a
specific time but a way of speaking of former time, equivalent in many
languages to "previously" or "at an earlier time."
 You yourselves is a possible translation of the Greek kai humeis;
or it could be "you, also (as well as other Gentiles)" (see TNT). An
equivalent of the emphatic you yourselves may be expressed in some
languages as "you are the very ones who." For live see 1.10, 2.6.
 According to such desires represents the Greek "in these" (see
RSV), the pronoun being read as neuter, referring to the sins or vices
of verses 5-6. Some, however, contend that if the longer text of verse
6 is read (that is, with the clause "upon those who do not obey him"),
then the pronoun is demonstrably masculine, meaning "among such people
you once lived," but this does not necessarily follow (see Lightfoot,
Beare, and others).
 Used to live according to such desires must often be restructured
so as to read "such desires controlled you," or "such desires caused you
to live as you did," or "because you had such desires, you lived as you
did."
 When your life was dominated by them: the Greek is literally "when
you lived in them" (RSV), but more would appear to be involved than
merely an exact repetition of the first part of the sentence. Though the
expression when your life was dominated by them does seem to involve more
than what is expressed in the previous statement, it is essentially a
means of emphasizing the previous clause, and accordingly it may be
possible to coalesce the two statements into a single one by making the
combined statement more emphatic. This may be done in some cases by
adding adverbial expressions such as "completely" or "entirely."

3.8   But now you must get rid of all these things:
       anger, passion, hateful feelings. No insults or
       obscene talk must ever come from your lips.

Now: TNT takes it not as simply temporal, but as a consequence of
the preceding argument, and translates "now as Christians" (see Note). But
it would appear that now is best interpreted as suggesting a contrast with
the temporal expression at one time in the previous verse.
 You must get rid of all these things must undergo rather considerable
change in some languages if the correct meaning is to be preserved. In
the first place, these things refer to actions and emotions, not to objects,
and you must get rid of must often be expressed as "you must no longer do"
or "you must stop doing." Such phrases can then be best linked directly
with the wrong attitudes or actions by saying "you must no longer be
angry."
 This verse lists five sins which the Colossians are to get rid of
(see the same verb in Rom 13.12; Eph 4.22,25; 1 Peter 2.1; James 1.21).

[81]

The first two are practically synonymous: anger and passion. Some commentators see the first (orgē) as the settled condition and the second one (thumos) as occasional outbursts of passion. Anger and passion are frequently expressed in metaphorical language. For example, anger may be referred to as "being hot in the face" or "burning in your heart," and passion is sometimes referred to as "exploding with anger" or "his heart is fighting."

Hateful feelings translates a Greek word which means "evil" or "wickedness" in its most general aspect. The more specific "malice" (RSV) is a possible interpretation (also Phps NEB NAB NIV). An ancient Greek lexicographer, Suidas, defined kakia thus: "the eagerness to harm one's neighbor"[9] (so Lightfoot, Peake). Kakia may thus be translated as "desire to do bad to others," or "desire to harm others," or "...cause them to suffer."

Insults (TEV) or "slander" (RSV and others) is abusive speech against someone by telling lies or otherwise insulting him. (The word may mean "blasphemy," that is, irreverent speech about God, but this meaning is hardly possible here). Since insulting is an element of universal behavior, there is generally no difficulty involved in finding an adequate term to express such actions. In some cases, however, a more descriptive expression may be used, for example, "saying bad things about people."

"Foul talk" (RSV) represents a Greek word which occurs only here in the NT (see a close parallel in Eph 5.4). NEB has "filthy talk," NAB NIV "filthy language."

Obscene talk may simply be expressed as "using words that should never be spoken" or as in some instances, "speaking taboo words."

Why "from your mouth" (RSV) is added is hard to tell, since the last sin mentioned is by definition a matter of speaking. It is not necessary to represent this phrase formally in translation as TEV and RSV have done; see JB Phps NEB NAB. Rather than from your lips many languages use "from you mouth," or "from your tongue," or "from your throat." It is, however, usually more natural to say "you must not insult people or use bad words," rather than to speak of insults and obscene talk "coming from one's lips."

3.9-10   Do not lie to one another, for you have put off the
         old self with its habits 10 and have put on the new
         self. This is the new being which God, its Creator,
         is constantly renewing in his own image, in order to
         bring you to a full knowledge of himself.

Do not lie to one another begins a long sentence which goes on to the end of verse 11. Paul is talking about relations within the Christian community. The prohibition is enforced by two considerations: you have put off the old...and have put on the new. The two verbs (apekduō and enduō) are used of taking off and putting on clothes. The language probably derives from the rite of baptism, in which a person took off his or her clothes before baptism and put on new, clean clothes after. Some take the two participles as imperatival in force and translate: "put off...and put on" (Lohse, TC GeCL). The verb "put off" occurs in 2.15; and for the cognate noun see 2.11.

The use of the figurative expressions of "putting off" and "putting on" for a type of behavior is often quite meaningful, but it may suggest that one's personality is something as external as clothing and may even be interpreted to mean that one's personality is a kind of disguise by which the true self is actually hidden. If such is the case, it may be important to shift the metaphor into another area of meaning, for example, "for you have gotten rid of the old self with its habits and you have acquired a new self."

The old self (TEV) or "the old nature" (RSV) represents literally "the old person," and refers to the readers' character before accepting the Christian message.

It may be quite difficult in some languages to speak of "the old self" and "the new self." Accordingly, the only way in which one can really speak of "putting off the old self" is by saying "ceasing to be what you used to be." Accordingly, "putting on the new self" may be rendered as "becoming a new kind of person."

Habits are "actions," or "deeds," or "practices" (RSV); see also Rom 8.13. With its habits may be expressed in some languages as "the way in which you used to behave" or "what you customarily did."

Reverting now to language derived from the creation account (Gen 1.26-27, see also 1 Cor 15.45-49), Paul says that God is constantly renewing this new being in his own image. It seems quite clear that the implied actor in the passive participle "is being renewed" (RSV) is God, and TEV has made this explicit. Some (SpCL FrCL) take it as middle, "which renews itself," but this does not seem very likely. For "renew," "to make new again," see also 2 Cor 4.16; for the cognate noun, see Rom 12.2, Titus 3.5.

This is the new being may be expressed in some instances as "this is the new you" or more frequently "you are this new person."

The appositional its Creator must often be expressed as a clause, for example, "God who created it" or "God who created you as a new person."

There are certain serious problems involved in a literal translation of constantly renewing, since this might imply that God is repeatedly destroying and remaking. Having already identified the believer as "a new person," it may be better then to render constantly renewing as "causing to be more and more like," for example, "this is the new kind of person which God who has created it is constantly causing to be more and more like himself."

In his own image: the renewal process has as its goal the complete restoration in the creature of the likeness of the creator. The creator is, at the same time, the one who renews, and this process restores the divine image which had been effaced by sin. For image see 1.15. A literal translation of in his own image can be seriously misinterpreted as the reference to an idol of God. Therefore, it may be important to translate in his own image as "like him" or "to act as he acts."

In order to bring you to a full knowledge of himself translates the Greek eis epignōsin. Some, like RSV, have simply "(being renewed) in knowledge," which is not very clear and which seems to miss the force of the preposition eis. Moule suggests that it may mean "that the process described results in knowledge or perception--that response of the whole person to God or Christ which is distinctive of the Christian experience"[10] (see also Beare). It seems better to take the preposition to indicate either purpose or result, rather than the element which is being renewed (as RSV suggests). Full knowledge: for epignōsis see 1.9,10. The object is not expressed, but it seems clearly to be God himself (Moule) or God's will (Lohse).

In order to bring you to a full knowledge of himself may be expressed as "in order to cause you to know him completely." Though the context may suggest mere "knowledge about God," it is more likely that the Greek term implies "experience of" or "coming into a relationship with," as occurs in so many other contexts, especially in Paul's writings.

3.11   As a result, there is no longer any distinction between
          Gentiles and Jews, circumcised and uncircumcised,
          barbarians, savages, slaves, and free men, but Christ
          is all, Christ is in all.

As a result translates the Greek adverb "where," which means "in this new situation," "in this new humanity (which God creates)." It may also be rendered as "because of this" or "because of what God has done." The verb that follows (see also 1 Cor 6.5, Gal 3.28, Col 3.11, James 1.17) may be either there is (not) (TEV) or as a stronger assertion "there cannot be" (RSV). In the new humanity, all racial, religious, national, and social distinctions are abolished (see also 1 Cor 12.13, Gal 3.28).

It may not be possible to render literally there is no longer any distinction between Gentiles and Jews... Instead of such an abstract word as distinction, it may be necessary to specifically contrast Gentiles and Jews, circumcised and uncircumcised, etc., for example, "because of what God has done, Gentiles are no different from Jews; circumcised people are no different from uncircumcised." Accordingly, the last four classes may be spoken of as "barbarians, savages, slaves, and free men are all the same."

The word "Greek" (RSV) stands for Gentiles as a whole, not just people from Greece; circumcised and uncircumcised is practically the same as Jews and Gentiles. If, as in so many instances, circumcised and uncircumcised can best be rendered as Jews and non-Jews (a phrase which likewise distinguishes "Jews and Gentiles"), it may be best to coalesce these two distinctions into one, for example, "Jews and non-Jews" or "those who are Jews and those who are not Jews."

Barbarians may simply be "foreigners" (Phps): it is the name that Greeks applied to all other races. Barbarians may often be translated as "those of other tribes" or "those who speak strange languages."

Savages represents the Greek "Scythian" (RSV), who were reputed by the Romans to be the wildest, most uncivilized, people living. Josephus said of them that they were little better than wild beasts. (This list does not include the sexual distinction "male and female," which appears in Gal 3.28.) Savages may be expressed as "uncivilized people," or idiomatically as "tribes living far away," or "people without farms" (an expression used in some languages to designate a relatively primitive type of hunting and gathering society).

Christ is all, Christ is in all is a summary way of stating that in the new humanity Christ is all that matters, since he is in all alike (in all could mean "in all things," but more probably means "in everyone," "in all people" who belong to the new humanity). NAB "Christ is everything in all of you," JB "There is only Christ: he is everything and he is in everything," Phps "Christ is all that matters, for Christ lives in all." Christ is all may also be expressed as "Christ is the one who is important." Expressed negatively, the same phrase may be rendered as "there is no one else except Christ who is important."

In rendering Christ is in all, it may be essential to specify who or what is involved in all. If all is to be interpreted as a reference to non-humans, then one could only say "Christ is in all the universe" or "...in all that exists," but since the more usual interpretation relates all to persons, it may be best to say "in all of you." If, however, one translates in all as "in all people," there are certain theological problems which immediately arise, since this would presuppose that in some measure Christ dwells in all human beings irrespective of their religious beliefs or relationship to God. This would seem to be quite contrary to what Paul is speaking of in this context.

3.12   You are the people of God; he loved you and chose you for his own. So then, you must clothe yourselves with compassion, kindness, humility, gentleness, and patience.

This verse, giving the five virtues which the Colossians are to put on, begins a sentence which continues in verse 13, with its emphasis upon the need for forgiveness, and ends with verse 14, which gives the sixth virtue, love, as the one which binds the other virtues in a perfect whole.

The imperative "put on" (RSV), with which the verse begins, is a consequence of what is said in verses 9-10 you have put off the old self... and have put on the new self. It is probably still the language of baptism, the fresh garment the baptized person puts on (see especially Gal 3.27). The imperative is justified by the fact that the Colossians are "God's chosen ones, holy and beloved" (RSV), terms used in the OT of Israel and applied in the NT to believers as the new Israel, the true people of God. TEV has changed the order, placing you are the people of God (RSV "holy") first (see 1.2). The expression he loved you translates the passive participle (RSV "beloved"), also used in 1 Thes 1.4, 2 Thes 2.13 (see also the passive adjective in Rom 11.28). The third, "God's chosen ones" (RSV), is also represented in TEV by the active he...chose you for his own (compare Rom 8.33).

There is an inherent problem of interpretation in a literal rendering of you are the people of God, for this could be interpreted in an exclusive sense, that is to say, that the believers in Colossae were the only people of God. It may, therefore, be necessary to say "you are part of the people of God" or "you belong to the people of God." On the other hand, a more natural exression in some languages is simply "you belong to God."

In choosing an appropriate term to render loved, especially in speaking of God's love for people, there may be a number of difficulties because of special connotations involved in local terms for "love." The three major distinctions in many languages are (1) love of parents for children (and sometimes conversely children for parents), (2) sexual love, and (3) love between friends. More often than not in speaking of God's love for people, a term related to parental love seems to be the most appropriate and the least likely to introduce wrong associations of meaning.

Chose you for his own may be expressed as "chose you in order that you could belong to him" or "chose you in order to possess you."

As in verses 9 and 10, it may not be possible to employ the figurative expression you must clothe yourselves with, since this might suggest something rather temporary and even superficial, that is to say, "putting on an outward appearance of something." Therefore, you must clothe yourselves with compassion, kindness, humility, gentleness, and patience must be rendered as "you must show compassion, kindness, humility, gentleness, and patience." In a number of languages, however, these five virtues cannot be expressed as nouns (see below).

On the basis of their status described by these three terms, the Colossians are to "clothe" themselves with five virtues: (1) compassion translates the biblical "bowels of mercy" (compare KJV), a feeling of sympathy for the needs and sufferings of others; (2) kindness (also 2 Cor 6.6, Gal 5.22, Eph 2.7) is a ready disposition to listen and respond to others; (3) humility is the recognition of the fact that all are of equal value in God's sight (see especially Phil 2.3), which makes it impossible for a Christian to be arrogant in his relation with a fellow Christian (see the contrasting false humility in 2.18,23); (4) gentleness (RSV "meekness") is closely allied to the previous virtues, and is a consequence of it (see Gal 6.1, 2 Tim 2.25); (5) patience, the attitude of forbearance and tolerance, is regularly listed as one of the prime Christian virtues (2 Cor 6.6, Gal 5.22, Eph 4.2, 2 Tim 3.10, 4.2).

Compassion is often expressed in figurative language, for example, "your heart should go out to others," or "you should feel sorrow in your heart for others," or "you should weep in your insides because of others."

Kindness may be expressed as "be kind to others" or "do good for others."

As in so many contexts, humility is best expressed as a negation of pride, for example, "do not be proud" or "do not think that you are better than other people."

Gentleness may likewise be expressed frequently as a negation of something that is wrong, for example, "do not be harsh in dealing with others" or "do not be hard in your thought toward others."

Patience may be expressed as "putting up with people a long time" or "suffering long because of people" and expressed negatively, "not being irritated with people."

3.13   Be tolerant with one another and forgive one another whenever any of you has a complaint against someone else. You must forgive one another just as the Lord has forgiven you.

The two participles "forbearing" and "forgiving" (RSV) further
characterize the attitude of Christians toward one another. As often
happens, the participles may be understood and translated as imperatives,
and not as dependent qualifying clauses. Be tolerant is of particular
relevance in dealing with people who are ignorant or weak (compare
especially 2 Cor 11.19). Be tolerant is very similar in meaning to patience
(verse 12). In some instances, one may be expressed positively and the
second negatively, for example, "putting up with people a long time" and
"not being irritated by people."

The word for complaint occurs only here in the NT (compare the cognate
verb memphomai "find fault with, blame" Rom 9.19, Heb 8.8). It may be
important to indicate that both the forgiveness and the complaints may be
reciprocal, for example, "you should forgive one another when you have
any complaints one against the other."

The command for them to forgive one another (for the verb charizomai
see 2.13) is directly related to the fact that the Lord has forgiven you
(see also Matt 6.14-15, Rom 15.7, Eph 4.32). The Lord here is clearly
Christ (some Greek mss in fact have "Christ"--see KJV).

Some languages employ quite different expressions depending upon
whether the object of the forgiveness is a sin or a person. For example,
one may speak of forgiving a sin as "wiping out the sin" or "throwing
away the guilt," but in "forgiving a person," it may be necessary to say
"to return a person's sin to him," or "to give back a person's sin," or
even "to accept a person again."

3.14 And to all these qualities add love, which binds
    all things together in perfect unity.

To all these qualities add love represents the Greek prepositional
phrase which has no verb, literally, "and on them love." The preposition
epi may simply be (1) local "on" or "over" (following the figure of
"clothing" in verse 12), (2) "in addition to" (Moule, TC Gpd JB NAB NIV),
(3) or a degree of comparison, "more than all these," "above all these"
(as RSV seems to mean, also Phps Mft TNT NEB Brc TOB FrCL). The Tagalog CL
translates, "Above all else, love one another, for this is the bond of
perfect unity." As noted in the Tagalog CL translation, love must be
treated as a verb, not as a noun referring to something which may be
"added." It may be, therefore, necessary in a number of instances to render
to all these qualities add love as "in addition to doing all that, you
must also love one another" or even more important than doing all that,
you should love one another."

Love is the normal NT word for God's or Christ's love for mankind,
and is taken to be the supreme Christian virtue (Rom 13.8-10, 1 Cor 12.31-
-13.13). It is here called "the bond of perfection, or completeness." The
word "bond" (sundesmos) appears in 2.19 as a "ligament" in the body. The
genitive "of perfection" can be understood as indicating result or purpose
(so Lohse, compare Turner Moulton III, 212, "the bond producing perfection").
But it seems more natural (even though nowhere else in the NT is this said
of love) that (1) it is love which binds all the Christian virtues together in perfect unity, or harmony, which gives order and coherence to

Christian character and conduct; or (2) it is love which binds all
Christians together in perfect harmony in the body of Christ, the Church
(Peake, Beare; FrCL GeCL).

As already suggested, it may be impossible to use a noun for love
which is spoken of as "doing something," that is to say, "binding all
things together." It is, however, possible in many instances to say "by
your loving one another, everything is brought together as one in a
perfect way," or on the basis of the second possible interpretation of
this passage, "by loving one another, you bind yourselves together as
though you are one and this is just as it should be." By saying "this is
just as it should be," one can express the concept of "perfection."

3.15 The peace that Christ gives is to guide you in the
decisions you make; for it is to this peace that God
has called you together in the one body. And be
thankful.

"The peace of Christ" (RSV) is quite evidently the peace that has
its origin in Christ, the peace that Christ gives (compare John 14.27,
Eph 2.14, 2 Thes 3.16), not the peace that Christ himself possesses. It
is the spirit of fellowship and harmony that must prevail in the Christian community. Some later manuscripts, whose copyists were perhaps influenced by the language of Phil 4.7, have "the peace of God" (compare
KJV). The peace that Christ gives is better expressed in a number of
languages as causative, for example, "the peace that Christ causes" or
"Christ is the one who causes you to be at peace with one another, and
this is to guide you..."

Is to guide you in the decisions you make translates the Greek "is
to judge in your hearts." The verb brabeuō occurs only here in the NT
(compare katabrabeuō in 2.18) and means "to serve as umpire; to determine, decide" a matter. After examining the way in which the word is
used elsewhere, Lightfoot says, "It appears that the idea of a decision
and an award is prominent in the word, and that it must not be taken to
denote simply rule or power."[11]

To guide you in the decisions you make may be expressed as "to
cause you to make decisions as to what you should do" or as expressed in
direct discourse, "this will cause you to decide,'We must do this!'"

The Greek "in your hearts" (RSV) is by some taken to mean the
locale, the place where the peace from Christ is to rule: it is an in-
terior reality, inside the person (compare Wey TC). Others, however, take
"heart" in the biblical sense of "mind, thinking," and so understand and
translate the passage as TEV has done, in the decisions you make (compare
Phps Brc). Thus understood, the following injuction is more fitting for
it is to this peace that God has called you together in the one body:
harmony and cooperation within the fellowship, the Church, was the intention of God when he called the Colossians to be his people.

In the one body is a reference to the Church (see 1.18). Some, however, believe that the absence of the definite article in Greek makes
the phrase mean "in one body," a reference to the local community. In
either case, the metaphor "body" is a significant one for Paul as the

best picture of the unity of Christians in union with Christ.

The clause for it is to this peace that God has called you together in the one body must be rather radically restructured in some languages, for example, "for God has called you together to be one body in order that you should experience this kind of peace."

The phrase in the one body must be identified in some languages as a figurative expression, "in order to form one body, as it were."

In translating the verb called, especially in this type of context, it is important to avoid certain connotations or aspects of meaning. For example, one would not wish to introduce the idea of "shouting at" or the implications of "commanding." In this type of context, called is much closer to the meaning of "to urge" or, as in some languages, "to urgently invite."

And be thankful, that is, to God: this command is added almost as an afterthought (only here does the adjective eucharistos occur in the NT); not only gratitude, but its expression in the giving of thanks to God is commanded (also verses 16b, 17b). The imperative expression be thankful can best be expressed in some languages as a type of obligation, for example, "you must be thankful to God" or "you should be thankful to God."

3.16   Christ's message in all its richness must live in
        your hearts. Teach and instruct one another with
        all wisdom. Sing psalms, hymns, and sacred songs;
        sing to God with thanksgiving in your hearts.

"The word of Christ" (RSV) is the Christian message, the gospel; it is the message about Christ. This is the only occurrence of this phrase in the NT. Some manuscripts have the more usual "the word of God" (as in 1.25) or "the word of the Lord." Since this message is about Christ and not a message which Christ himself uttered, it would be better even in English to use a phrase "the message about Christ."

Live translates the Greek "be at home" (enoikeō: of the Holy Spirit, Rom 8.11, 2 Tim 1.14; of faith, 2 Tim 1.5; of sin, Rom 7.17; see also oikeō en, of the Holy Spirit, Rom 8.9,11; 1 Cor 3.16). The meaning of the command is that the Christian message must be an integral and permanent living force in them, not just an outward performance or routine activities. It may be rather difficult in some languages to speak of "a message living in someone's heart." However, a rendering such as "a message finding a place in a person's heart" may be acceptable or "a message may speak to someone's heart."

In all its richness is a metaphor for all the resources and blessings which are to be found in the Christian message. The phrase in all its richness may characterize either the message or the way in which the message must live in the believer. The meaning is essentially the same in either case. In the first instance, one may speak of the "the wonderful message" and in the second instance, "must live in a wonderful way."

In your hearts represents one meaning of the Greek "in you" (RSV) but the phrase could mean "among you," that is, in the fellowship of the Church. If the second interpretation is accepted, one may translate "must live in you" as "must influence how you live with one another" or "must determine how you behave toward one another."

What follows in the Greek text may be variously understood: (1) the three participles "teaching...admonishing...singing" may be understood as circumstantial, expressing the circumstances in which the command of the main verb is carried out; or they may be taken as imperatives, as so often occurs in the NT. (2) With all wisdom may go either with the preceding "living" or with the following "teaching and admonishing"; most prefer the latter (for the former, see KJV TC Gpd Mft). (3) Psalms, hymns, and sacred songs may go with what precedes, that is, with the verbs "instructing and admonishing," by means of psalms, etc. (so Lightfoot, KJV Mft Gpd TC Wey); or they may go with the following participle "singing" (RSV TEV and most other modern translations).

Instruct: the verb noutheteō means "warn, admonish, instruct"; see "warn" in 1.28; here it could mean "warn." In view of the usefulness in distinguishing between teach and instruct, it may be best here to translate "teach one another and warn one another." A more positive rendering of instruct may be expressed figuratively as "show the right road to one another."

The phrase with all wisdom may be rendered as means, for example, "by using all wisdom" or "by being wise in every way."

As commentators point out, it is impossible precisely to differentiate between the three terms that follow (all three also in Eph 5.19): psalms are OT psalms, used also by Christians in their corporate worship; hymns could be specifically Christian compositions in honor of Jesus as Lord and Savior; and "spiritual songs" (RSV) could be spontaneous outbursts of inspired singing, prompted by the Spirit (compare Brc).

Psalms may be referred to as "songs of the Scriptures," and hymns could be designated as "songs about Jesus." Similarly, "spiritual songs" could be translated as "songs from God's Spirit" or "songs caused by the Spirit."

With thanksgiving translates the Greek "in grace." The understanding of this phrase is made difficult by the textual problem of whether or not the definite article ("in the grace") belongs to the text. (UBS GK NT gives hardly any help by including it within brackets.) It could be (1) "with thanksgiving" as TEV and RSV take it (compare Abbott, Lohse; see NEB TNT JB NAB etc.); or (2) "by the grace (of God)" (Lightfoot); or (3) "with beauty" (Beare).

It may be difficult in some languages to speak of "singing to God with thanksgiving." "Sing" and "give thanks" are different, though closely related, activities. It may be possible to treat them as coordinate, for example, "sing to God and be thankful," but it may also be more natural to express the singing as dependent on the thanksgiving, for example, "when you sing to God, be thankful."

In your hearts may be associated with thanksgiving (as RSV TEV and others do; Brc has "heartfelt"), or with the third participle "singing," in which case it could be taken to mean "singing with all your hearts," fervently, enthusiastically (so FcCL Brc Phps NAB Gpd). It is hardly likely that Paul meant that the singing was to be silent, and not vocal. Though it seems quite natural in English to speak of being "thankful in your hearts" or "singing with all your heart," it may seem quite strange in some languages to associate "heart" with either thanksgiving or singing. For example, one may wish to speak of "being thankful in your thoughts" or "have your mind say thanks to God," while "singing with all your heart" would be expressed as "singing with strength" or "with great happiness."

Instead of to God, some later manuscripts, influenced by the parallel in Eph 5.19, have "to the Lord" (KJV).

3.17   Everything you do or say, then, should be done in the name of the Lord Jesus, as you give thanks through him to God the Father.

This verse brings this section (3.5-17) to a close with a general command that everything the Colossians do and say must be in the name of the Lord Jesus, that is, as his committed and obedient followers and representatives. In the name of the Lord Jesus may be expressed most satisfactorily in a number of languages as "as believers in the Lord Jesus" or "as followers of the Lord Jesus." The passive construction should be done may cause certain difficulties, especially in languages where an active expression must be employed. In such cases one may be able to translate "whatever you do and whatever you say, you should do and say in the name of the Lord Jesus." Sometimes the meaning of "whatever you say and whatever you do" must be rendered as a condition, for example, "if you do anything and if you say anything, then you should do and say all that in the name of the Lord Jesus."

Through him, that is, through Christ, means that their thanksgiving to God must recognize that Christ is the medium through which all their blessings have come from God. A literal rendering of the phrase through him might suggest that the believers were to give thanks to God only through Christ as a kind of intermediary, that is to say, that the believers should pray to Christ in order that he would then communicate the thanks to God. In reality, of course, the believer is to give thanks to God the Father because of what has happened through Christ, and it may be necessary to make this explicit, for example, "as you thank God the Father for what has happened to you through Christ" or "...for what Christ has done for you."

As you give thanks translates a participle, which some take, as elsewhere, to function as an imperative. Instead of to God the Father, some later manuscripts, influenced by the parallel in Eph 5.20, have "to the God and Father" (see KJV). As in other contexts, it may be necessary to translate to God the Father as "to God who is our Father."

| | TEV | (3.18--4.1) | RSV |

PERSONAL RELATIONS IN THE NEW LIFE

TEV	RSV
18 Wives, submit yourselves to your husbands, for that is what you should do as Christians. 19 Husbands, love your wives	18 Wives, be subject to your husbands, as is fitting in the Lord. 19 Husbands, love your wives, and do not be harsh with them. 20

[91]

and do not be harsh with them.
20 Children, it is your
Christian duty to obey your
parents always, for that is
what pleases God.
21 Parents, do not irritate
your children, or they will
become discouraged.
22 Slaves, obey your human
masters in all things, not only
when they are watching you because you want to gain their
approval; but do it with a
sincere heart because of your
reverence for the Lord. 23 Whatever you do, work at it with
all your heart, as though you
were working for the Lord and
not for men. 24 Remember that
the Lord will give you as a
reward what he has kept for
his people. For Christ is the
real Master you serve. 25 And every
wrongdoer will be repaid for the
wrong things he does, because
God judges everyone by the same
standard.
4 Masters, be fair and just
in the way you treat your slaves.
Remember that you too have a
Master in heaven.

Children, obey your parents in
everything, for this pleases the
Lord. 21 Fathers, do not provoke
your children, lest they become
discouraged. 22 Slaves, obey in
everything those who are your
earthly masters, not with eyeservice,
as men-pleasers, but in singleness
of heart, fearing the Lord. 23
Whatever your task, work heartily,
as serving the Lord and not men,
24 knowing that from the Lord you
will receive the inheritance as
your reward; you are serving the
Lord Christ. 25 For the wrongdoer
will be paid back for the wrong he
has done, and there is no partiality.
4 Masters, treat your slaves
justly and fairly, knowing that you
also have a Master in heaven.

From the way in which this section suddenly begins (without any
logical reference to what precedes) and from its style, scholars conclude
that what we have here is taken, or adapted, by Paul from a traditional
list already formulated by Christian teachers. For similar lists see
Eph 5.22--6.9, 1 Peter 2.18--3.7, 1 Tim 2.8-15, 6.1-2, Titus 2.1-10. There
are three sets of relations in the household, with reciprocal duties and
responsibilities: wives and husbands (3.18-19), children and parents
(3.20-21), and slaves and masters (3.22--4.1).

3.18   Wives, submit yourselves to your husbands, for
     that is what you should do as Christians.

Submit yourselves represents the Greek hupotassomai, a term used
in military contexts of a subordinate's relationship to his superior in
the army hierarchy. It is used of a wife's relation to her husband in
Eph 5.22, Titus 2.5, 1 Peter 3.1, of servants to masters, Titus 2.9, 1
Peter 2.13, of people to state authorities, Rom 13.1. It means "to be
subject to, obey, be ruled by." It carries the implication of subordination,

reflecting the standards of the time, which no amount of special pleading can banish. Phps "adapt yourselves" is an unfortunate attempt to make the command more tolerable in a different age.

A literal translation of wives in direct address may seem not only unusual but almost depreciating in some languages. A more satisfactory equivalent may be "you women who are married."

Submit yourselves must be rendered in such a way as to avoid any connotations of sexual submission. In some instances, the most appropriate equivalent is "acknowledge your husbands as being the ones who give orders" or "recognize your husbands as leaders in the family" or "...chiefs in the household." It is also, of course, possible to simply translate "obey your husbands."

That is what you should do as Christians translates the Greek "as is proper in the Lord" (for other examples of the impersonal anēkō see Eph 5.4, Philemon 8). The Christian wife's relation to her husband is determined by her status "as a Christian," which is what the Greek prepositional phrase "in the Lord" means.

As Christians may be rendered as "as persons who are followers of Christ," but this phrase is often more satisfactorily interpreted as a type of cause, for example, "since you are followers of Christ" or "because you have put your trust in Christ."

3.19   Husbands, love your wives and do not be harsh with them.

Love (compare 3.14). Though in this context love relates to the relationship between husband and wife, it should not focus upon sexual attraction but upon "tender care for," equivalent in some languages to "show tender appreciation for." As in the case of wives, it may also be important to address husbands as "you men who are married."

Unless the translation is carefully worded, it may in some languages suggest that a husband should have more than one wife (the same type of problem may also occur in verse 18); therefore, it may be necessary to translate husbands, love your wives as "each of you husbands should love his wife." Similarly, then, in the second part of the sentence the translation should read, "do not be harsh with her."

Be harsh translates the verb pikrainō, "to make bitter," used literally in Rev 8.11, 10.9, 10. Here it is used figuratively "be embittered against, be cruel to, be harsh with" (so most translations). Do not be harsh may be rendered idiomatically as "do not treat her like a maid" or "do not make a slave of her."

3.20   Children, it is your Christian duty to obey your parents always, for that is what pleases God.

TEV your Christian duty represents the prepositional phrase en kuriō which appears in Greek at the end of the verse. The whole Greek phrase "is pleasing in the Lord" is unusual and does not seem to be exactly equal to the normal dative phrase "pleasing to the Lord" (Eph 5.10). The word "pleasing" is here in Greek (euareston) probably to be taken absolutely, that is, "pleasing to God," and the prepositional phrase en kuriō may be taken in the same way as it is taken in verse 18 (see Lightfoot, Moule). So TEV represents en kuriō by your Christian duty and euareston by what pleases God. NEB has "that is pleasing to God and is the Christian way," TNT "this is pleasing to God and is what Christians should do"; see also Brc FrCL.

Your Christian duty must sometimes be rephrased as "as Christians you should" or "since you are Christians, you must."

In a number of languages, there are quite distinct words for children depending upon the age. The most frequent distinctions involve (1) babies before they are weaned, (2) small children before they can talk satisfactorily, (3) children from the age of speaking until puberty, and (4) adolescents from the age of puberty until marriage. Probably the most satisfactory term is one which would designate children between the age of speaking until the age of puberty, though if at all possible, a more general expression should be employed.

Though in the Greek text the term parents refers specifically to father and mother, it seems rather anomalous in some languages to speak of "obeying your father and mother," when in reality children are normally expected to obey the mother and the maternal uncle, that is to say, the brother of the mother. It is not advisable to try to introduce a cultural adaptation by introducing "mother and mother's brother," but it may be useful to employ a term for parents which designages a somewhat wider class of adults in the extended family.

3.21   Parents, do not irritate your children, or they will become discouraged.

Parents is how TEV translates hoi pateres (also JB BJ TOB); all others have "fathers." The plural of the word for "father" may be used in the sense of "parents" (see Heb 11.23); but the more common word for "parents" is used in verse 20, and it probably is true that in this verse it is the fathers who are being addressed, not both the fathers and the mothers.

In place of the vocative expression parents, it may be appropriate in some languages to use a qualifying clause, for example, "you who have children."

Irritate translates erethizō "to provoke, nag, embitter, make resentful." The situation envisaged seems to be that of the father constantly correcting and reprimanding the child for every little wrong or imagined wrong. It may be important to make more explicit the significance of irritate, for example, "to make your children bitter by always complaining about what they do" or "do not make your children angry by always criticizing them for everything they do."

Discouraged translates a Greek word found only here in the NT; in this context, it means that the child feels that he can never do anything right and so gives up trying.

Discouraged may often be expressed idiomatically as "they will no longer have a heart," "they will close their minds to everything," or "they will hide inside of themselves."

3.22   Slaves, obey your human masters in all things,
             not only when they are watching you because you want
             to gain their approval; but do it with a sincere
             heart because of your reverence for the Lord.

It should be noticed that in contrast with the instructions to
wives, husbands, parents, children, and masters, each of which takes only
one short sentence, the instructions to slaves takes four verses. This
may be due to the fact that there were more problems arising from a
Christian slave's relationship to his master (Christian and non-Christian)
than from any other social relationship of the time.

Your human masters is literally "your masters according to the
flesh," so designated because they are contrasted to the supreme master,
the Lord (verse 24). In English the phrase human masters makes sense
because there is the implication that Christians have a heavenly master,
but if masters is translated as "those who own you," then it seems not
only strange but even ludicrous to talk about "human beings who own you,"
since a slave would never be owned by an animal. Under such circumstances,
human masters can simply be rendered as "those who own you," or "those
persons to whom you belong," or "those whom you must serve."

When they are watching you translates the Greek phrase "in eyeservice" (the noun is found only here and in Eph 6.6), meaning service
performed while being watched by the master, contrasted with genuine
service well performed, whether or not the master is watching.

You want to gain their approval translates the Greek compound word
"men-pleasers" (RSV). It may mean human approval in general; probably here
it has the masters in view, again in contrast with service that is
performed in order to please the divine master. A literal rendering of
they are watching you because you want to gain their approval may result
in complete misunderstanding. The clause because you want to gain their
approval does not relate to when they are watching you but to the matter
of obeying. It may be necessary, therefore, to shift the order of certain
of the clauses, for example, "because you want to gain their approval,
do not obey them merely when they are watching you."

A sincere heart translates "in singleness of heart," that is,
sincerely, honestly, with no ulterior motive or hidden intention. A sincere
heart may be rendered as "with your heart exposed," or "with people being
able to see what is in your heart," or "with your mind like a paper that
can be read."

Reverence stands for the participle "fearing" (RSV): it is that
sense of awe, reverence, fear, that in the OT specially characterizes
the attitude of the devout member of the believing community toward God.
Your reverence for the Lord may be expressed in some languages as "the
way in which you regard the Lord" or "the way in which you look upon the
greatness of the Lord." In this way, one may suggest something of the
"awe" which is to be understood in such a context.

The Lord is here the Lord Jesus Christ. Some manuscripts have "God"
(see KJV), but this seems an obvious conformance to the OT expression,
where "Lord" is Yahweh, that is, God. As in a number of contexts, the
Lord must be rendered as "our Lord," and in some languages it may be

necessary to add "Jesus" in order to avoid confusion with the OT references to God.

3.23   Whatever you do, work at it with all your heart, as though you were working for the Lord and not for men.

With all your heart (TEV) or "heartily" (RSV) translates the Greek ek psuchēs "from the soul." The reason Christian slaves should perform their duties in this manner is that they should consider their service as performed for the Lord Jesus Christ, and not only for their human masters.

In place of the phrase with all your heart, it may be more in keeping with the context to employ a phrase such as "with all your strength." Working for the Lord and not for men may be expressed as "working to help the Lord and not to help just men."

3.24   Remember that the Lord will give you as a reward what he has kept for his people. For Christ is the real Master you serve.

The first part of this verse is the concluding part of the sentence begun with verse 23, and further reinforces the command to Christian slaves to render genuine service to their human masters. The participle "knowing" (RSV) can be translated "because you know" or "since you know." In English the verb remember does not mean in this type of context that one has necessarily forgotten and later needs to have this called to mind. Rather, it suggests that the person should continue to bear something in mind. Therefore, one may begin verse 24 with the imperative "bear in mind" or "constantly realize."

The Lord will give you (TEV) has transformed the passive structure in Greek (RSV "from the Lord you will receive") into an active form.

As a reward what he has kept for his people translates the Greek "the reward of the inheritance," in which the genitive "of the inheritance" defines what "the reward" is. For the word "inheritance" see in 1.12 the discussion of klēros "lot." The reward consists of those blessings which God will bestow on his people; so instead of kept the meaning could be expressed by "promised."

In some languages, a reward is "a special payment," or "a payment over and above," or "an unexpected payment," that is to say, something which the person will receive in addition to the food and lodging which he receives as a slave.

For Christ is the real Master you serve translates a text which is variously interpreted: (1) the verb "to serve" may be read as an indicative, "you are serving" (so Lightfoot, Beare; TNT NIV Brc Phps Gpd SpCL FrCL GeCL TOB), or as an imperative, "you are to serve" (Moule, Lohse, Abbott, Peake; NEB); or (2) the Greek text (literally "to the Lord Christ") can be read "the Lord Christ" (RSV), which is an unusual expression (Rom 16.18 "our Lord Christ" is not identical). Most take "Christ" here as being in apposition to "the Lord," so that the phrase means "Christ is the Lord (or Master) you serve": so GeCL SpCL FrCL TOB Gpd NEB Brc; or else "Christ the Lord" (JB NAB).

In this context, the translation of master depends largely upon the way in which masters is rendered in verse 22. If, for example, masters in verse 22 is rendered as "those to whom you belong," then in verse 24 master may be rendered as "the one to whom you belong." The entire clause may then be stated as "for Christ is the one to whom you really belong and whom you serve" or "...and the one whom you work for."

3.25   And every wrongdoer will be repaid for the wrong things he does, because God judges everyone by the same standard.

The injuction to the slaves closes with a statement which, though directed specifically to them, may have a broader application, with both slaves and masters in view. Wrongdoer translates a participle "one who does evil," "one who wrongs (another)."

Will be repaid (for other places where this verb occurs see Matt 25.27, 2 Cor 5.10): the future refers to the Day of Judgement.

A literal translation of will be repaid might suggest that a wrongdoer will actually be compensated for his wrongs. It may, therefore, be necessary to translate will be repaid as "will have to suffer" or "will be punished," but in order to suggest that the punishment is somehow related to the degree of wrong, one may translate the first clause of verse 25 as "everyone who does wrong will be punished in proportion to the wrong things he has done."

God judges everyone by the same standard translates the Greek "there is no partiality" (RSV). For the noun see Rom 2.11, Eph 6.9, James 2.1; see also Acts 10.34, 1 Peter 1.17; for a similar statement in the OT see Deut 10.17, Psa 62.12. At the Day of Judgement God will not show favoritism or partiality to anyone, but will apply the same standard to all.

Serious misunderstandings have arisen as the result of literally translating this last clause in accordance with more traditional renderings. For example, a literal translation of the KJV "there is no respect of persons" has resulted in renderings which suggest that God pays no attention to people. Some translators have rendered "there is not partiality" (RSV) as "God has no special friends." In a strictly idiomatic context, this might be satisfactory, but it has been interpreted to mean that God is not really friendly with anyone. Even a literal translation of God judges everyone by the same standard could suggest that everyone receives precisely the same sentence. In some instances, one may use some such expression as "God uses the same measuring stick when he decided whether people have been good or bad." In a number of languages, however, lack of favoritism or partiality is expressed idiomatically, for example, "God doesn't look on people's faces when he is judging their hearts," or "God pays no attention to people's reputations when he judges what they have really done," or "whether a man is big in people's eyes makes no difference to God when he judges."

4.1   Masters, be fair and just in the way you treat your slaves. Remember that you too have a Master in heaven.

As commentators point out, there were probably very few Christian

4.1

slave-owners at the time. Be fair and just translates two words meaning "the right thing" and "the fair thing." The command to them is enforced by the reminder that they too are slaves of the Master in heaven. (Phps "you employers" is an unwarranted modernization of the text.) In place of a literal translation of be fair and just in the way you treat your slaves, it may be more satisfactory to say "treat your slaves in a fair and just way."

As in verse 24, remember signifies "bear in mind" or "continually keep in mind."

It may be quite impossible in some languages to say "you too have a Master in heaven." People do not "possess masters"; rather they "belong to masters" or "masters possess them." Accordingly, remember that you too have a Master in heaven may be translated as "bear in mind that you belong to one in heaven" or "bear in mind that the one who owns you is in heaven."

	TEV	(4.2-6)	RSV

INSTRUCTIONS

2 Be persistent in prayer, and keep alert as you pray, giving thanks to God. 3 At the same time pray also for us, so that God will give us a good opportunity to preach his message about the secret of Christ. For that is why I am now in prison. 4 Pray, then, that I may speak, as I should, in such a way as to make it clear.

5 Be wise in the way you act toward those who are not believers, making good use of every opportunity you have. 6 Your speech should always be pleasant and interesting, and you should know how to give the right answer to everyone.

2 Continue steadfastly in prayer, being watchful in it with thanksgiving; 3 and pray for us also, that God may open to us a door for the word, to declare the mystery of Christ, on account of which I am in prison, 4 that I may make it clear, as I ought to speak.

5 Conduct yourselves wisely toward outsiders, making the most of the time. 6 Let your speech always be gracious, seasoned with salt, so that you may know how you ought to answer every one.

This section is comprised of general admonitions concerning prayer (verses 2-4) and the Colossians' relations toward non-Christians, both in behavior (verse 5) and speech (verse 6).

<u>4.2</u>   Be persistent in prayer, and keep alert as you pray, giving thanks to God.

For similar injunctions to be persistent in prayer see Rom 12.12, Eph 6.18, Phil 4.6, 1 Thes 5.17. Be persistent in prayer may be rendered as "continue to pray," but more often than not a more satisfactory equivalent is "do not stop praying."

Besides being persistent, they are to keep alert. It is difficult to know precisely what this means; it does not seem probable that it is meant literally, "keep awake" (JB), but rather metaphorically, "with

[98]

mind awake" as NEB puts it, or else, as Beare suggests, "being watchful
against temptation." Keep alert as you pray may possibly be expressed as
"pay attention to what you are saying to God."

Once more giving thanks to God is stressed as an integral part of
all Christian prayer.

4.3　　　At the same time pray also for us, so that God will
　　　　give us a good opportunity to preach his message
　　　　about the secret of Christ. For that is why I am
　　　　now in prison.

Verse 3 is a continuation of the sentence that begins with verse 2
and ends with verse 4.

At the same time must not be rendered in such a way as to suggest
that everyone is to pray "at the same time." A more satisfactory
rendering in some languages is "whenever you pray, pray also for us." Us
here probably means Paul and his colleagues; some, however (compare Lohse,
GeCL), take it to refer only to Paul. God will give us a good opportunity
to preach his message translates "God may open for us a door for the
word." For the figure of "opening a door" see also 1 Cor 16.9, 2 Cor 2.12.
The apostle wants God to give him another opportunity to proclaim the
Christian message.

The purpose expressed in the clause so that God will give us a
good opportunity to preach his message may undergo certain restructuring,
for example, "so that God will allow us to preach his message freely" or
"...openly." In this way one may reproduce the meaning of good opportunity.

His message refers of course to the message which comes from God.
This is the message which the apostles were commissioned to proclaim.

This "word" is defined as the secret (or "mystery") of Christ (for
which see 1.26,27; 2.2), which is here almost a technical term for the
Christian message. The order of constituents in the phrase about the
secret of Christ may be appropriately altered in some instances, for in
a sense it is God's message about Christ, and it is the content of this
message which was kept secret. Therefore, one may render his message about
the secret of Christ as "God's message about Christ, a message which has
not been previously known."

It was because Paul had insisted on preaching the gospel that he
was in prison. The Greek verb "I am bound" does not necessarily mean that
Paul was in chains, but simply that he was not free (see, however, 4.18,
where "chains" are mentioned). Nowhere in this letter does Paul say where
he is in prison.

In the clause for that is why I am now in prison, the pronoun that
may have a rather vague reference or may be too far removed from the
reference of preaching. Furthermore, in the first part of verse 3, the
preaching is something in the future for which Paul is asking prayers. It
would not be a specific reason for Paul's being in prison. Accordingly,
it may be necessary to say "because I preached God's message, I am now
in prison."

4.4　　　Pray, then, that I may speak, as I should, in such a
　　　　way as to make it clear.

Here Paul asks his readers to pray that he may fulfill his duty of making clear the meaning of the secret of Christ, the Christian message. The same verb is here used as "revealed" in 1.26. Paul must not only proclaim the message, but also "expound its deeper implications" (Beare).

The necessity implied in as I should (TEV) or "as I ought" (RSV) comes from God, who laid upon Paul the responsibility of proclaiming the gospel. A literal rendering of that I may speak, as I should, might suggest merely that Paul is asking the Colossian Christians to pray for him to be able to speak clearly or to enunciate well the message. What Paul is praying for is the ability to proclaim the message in such a way as to make it clear, and it is this proclamation of the message which is his obligation. Therefore, it may be more appropriate to render verse 4 as "therefore pray that I may announce this message in such a way as to make it clear, for that is what I must do."

4.5   Be wise in the way you act toward those who are not believers, making good use of every opportunity you have.

The verb act is the same one used in 1.10, 2.6, 3.7, indicating way of life, behavior, conduct. Be wise in the way you act may be rendered as "behave wisely," or "use wisdom in the way in which you conduct yourself," or "be wise in the way in which you live."

The "outsiders" (RSV) are non-Christians (see the same designation in 1 Thes 4.12, 1 Cor 5.12-13, Mark 4.11). Since in some languages one must specify what is believed in, it may be necessary to render those who are not believers as "those who do not believe in Christ."

The participle that follows is literally "buying out, redeeming"; only here and in the parallel Eph 5.16 is it used in the sense of making good use of. Most commentators and translators give the same meaning as it appears in TEV and RSV. Some, however, have understood the text to mean "redeeming the time from the power of Evil," but this seems most unlikely. The Colossians are enjoined to seize and use every opportunity of witnessing to their faith to the non-Christian society in which they live.

In a number of languages, one must specify what is involved in every opportunity. Therefore, one may employ some such rendering as "make good use of every chance you have to speak to nonbelievers" or "use every opportunity well to show that you are believers."

4.6   Your speech should always be pleasant and interesting, and you should know how to give the right answer to everyone.

Continuing his admonition about relations with non-Christians, Paul says that the Colossians' conversation with them should always be pleasant. The phrase en chariti means "charming, pleasant, attractive."

Your speech does not refer to enunciation or pronunciation but to the content of what is said. Therefore, it may be more appropriate to translate "your words" or "when you talk with people, what you say should be pleasant and interesting."

The next phrase, "seasoned with salt" (RSV), is understood to mean that their conversation should be witty, interesting, pointed, not insipid or dull. And finally their conversation should always be adapted to the needs of everyone with whom they speak of the Christian message (for a similar idea see 1 Peter 3.15).

Rather than talking about words being "pleasant and interesting," many languages relate these characteristics to the response of persons who receive the communication, for example, "people should always be pleased and interested in what you say" or "what you say should always cause people to be pleased and interested."

Some rendering of the right answer may suggest "the polite answer," for in many societies a polite response is the correct one, not necessarily a true response. In some instances, one may render the second clause of verse 6 as "you should know how to answer everyone as you should" or "you should know how to answer everyone in a true way."

	TEV	(4.7-18)	RSV

FINAL GREETINGS

7 Our dear brother Tychicus, who is a faithful worker and fellow servant in the Lord's work, will give you all the news about me. 8 That is why I am sending him to you, in order to cheer you up by telling you how all of us are getting along. 9 With him goes Onesimus, that dear and faithful brother, who belongs to your group. They will tell you everything that is happening here.

10 Aristarchus, who is in prison with me, sends you greetings, and so does Mark, the cousin of Barnabas. (You have already received instructions to welcome Mark if he comes your way.) 11 Joshua, also called Justus, sends greetings too. These three are the only Jewish converts who work with me for the kingdom of God, and they have been a great help to me.

12 Greetings from Epaphras, another member of your group and a servant of Christ Jesus. He always prays fervently for you, asking God to make you stand firm, as mature and fully convinced

7 Tychicus will tell you all about my affairs; he is a beloved brother and faithful minister and fellow servant in the Lord. 8 I have sent him to you for this very purpose, that you may know how we are and that he may encourage your hearts, 9 and with him Onesimus, the faithful and beloved brother, who is one of yourselves. They will tell you of everything that has taken place here.

10 Aristarchus my fellow prisoner greets you, and Mark the cousin of Barnabas (concerning whom you have received instructions--if he comes to you, receive him), 11 and Jesus who is called Justus. These are the only men of the circumcision among my fellow workers for the kingdom of God, and they have been a comfort to me. 12 Epaphras, who is one of yourselves, a servant^g of Christ Jesus, greets you, always remembering you earnestly in his prayers, that you may stand mature and fully assured in all the will of God. 13 For I bear him witness that he has worked hard for you and for those in

Christians, in complete obedience to God's will. 13 I can personally testify to his hard work for you and for the people in Laodicea and Hierapolis. 14 Luke, our dear doctor, and Demas send you their greetings.

15 Give our best wishes to the brothers in Laodicea and to Nympha and the church that meets in her house.[f] 16 After you read this letter, make sure that it is read also in the church at Laodicea. At the same time, you are to read the letter that the brothers in Laodicea will send you. 17 And tell Archippus, "Be sure to finish the task you were given in the Lord's service."

18 With my own hand I write this: Greetings from Paul. Do not forget my chains!

May God's grace be with you.

Laodicea and in Hierapolis. 14 Luke the beloved physician and Demas greet you. 15 Give my greetings to the brethren at Laodicea, and to Nympha and the church in her house. 16 And when this letter has been read among you, have it read also in the church of the Laodiceans; and see that you read also the letter from Laodicea. 17 And say to Archippus, "See that you fulfil the ministry which you have received in the Lord."

18 I, Paul, write this greeting with my own hand. Remember my fetters. Grace be with you.

[g]Or slave

[f]Nympha...her house; some manuscripts have Nymphas...his house.

The final section of the letter is taken up with personal messages and greetings, which may be thus divided: (1) Tychicus and Onesimus are taking the letter to Colossae and will give the Colossians all the news about Paul and his companions (verses 7-9); (2) greetings are sent from six individuals who are with Paul (verses 10-14); (3) greetings are sent to the believers in Laodicea, to Nympha and the church in her house; instructions are given about exchanging letters with the Laodiceans; and a personal message is sent to Archippus (verses 14-17); (4) closing salutation, personally written by Paul (verse 18).

4.7   Our dear brother Tychicus, who is a faithful worker and fellow servant in the Lord's work, will give you all the news about me.

Tychicus (see Acts 20.4, Eph 6.21, 2 Tim 4.12, Titus 3.12) is called a dear brother and a faithful worker and fellow servant in the Lord's work. It is assumed that he is the same one who in Acts 20.4 appears as a companion of Paul, and who was from the province of Asia (of which Ephesus was the capital).

In the phrase our dear brother Tychicus, the order of constituents must be altered if the phrase is to be meaningful and natural in certain other languages, for example, "Tychicus, our fellow believer, who is dear to us." Dear may also be expressed as "whom we like very much" or "whom we so greatly appreciate."

Faithful worker could be "trustworthy helper"; the noun used is diakonos (as in 1.7,23). Faithful worker may be rendered as "a worker who can be trusted" or even "our helper whom we trust."

Fellow servant is used also of Epaphras in 1.7. The Greek "in the Lord" (RSV) may mean, as TEV has, in the Lord's work, or it may simply be a way of saying "Christian," which is so obvious, however, as not to need stating. Fellow servant in the Lord's work may be rendered as "one who serves the Lord along with us."

All the news about me are matters which Paul does not elaborate in the letter but leaves to Tychicus to deliver orally. (It is implied that Tychicus would be taking the letter to Colossae, but this is not stated explicitly, unless the verb "I am sending" in verse 8 means, as it sometimes does, "with the letter.") Will give you all the news about me may be expressed as "will tell you all that has happened to me" or "...all that has happened to me recently."

4.8   That is why I am sending him to you, in order to cheer you up by telling you how all of us are getting along.

I am sending translates what is called the epistolary aorist, that is, it looks at the action from the point of view of the recipients as they read the letter (RSV "I have sent" could be understood to mean Tychicus had been sent before Paul wrote to the Colossians).

Languages differ considerably in the way in which they treat tense forms in letters. Sometimes the tense forms depend upon the time of the writing; in other instances, the time of the receiving of the letter, that is to say, the way in which the letter is read. In still other instances, am sending in this context may be expressed as a future since Paul would be sending Tychicus presumably after he had finished the writing. In order to avoid serious misunderstanding, it is important to adjust the tense forms to the requirements of the language in to which a translation is being made.

Cheer you up or "encourage you" (see RSV): the same language as in 2.2. The rendering cheer you up implies that the believers in Colossae had become discouraged or at least apprehensive about what they had heard concerning Paul. Therefore, it may be appropriate to translate cheer you up as "cause you to be happy again" or, as expressed figuratively in some languages, "cause your heart to return."

"You may know how we are" (RSV) represents the best form of the text. Some manuscripts, however, have "he may know how you are" (compare KJV "he might know your estate"; Mft), for which see Metzger Textual Commentary, page 626. How all of us are getting along may be expressed as "what is happening to all of us" or "what all of us are experiencing."

4.9   With him goes Onesimus, that dear and faithful brother,
who belongs to your group. They will tell you everything that is happening here.

For Onesimus, see Philemon 10-20. Here he is simply referred to as
that dear and faithful brother, who belongs to your group. This quite
clearly means that he is from Colossae and would also appear to mean (as
in the case of Epaphras, verse 12) that he is a member of the church there.
But Beare, in the light of Philemon, says he was not yet a member of the
church.
    With him goes Onesimus may be expressed as "Onesimus will accompany
him" or "..."will travel with him."
    That dear and faithful brother may be translated as "he is a fellow
believer who is very dear to us and who can be trusted" or "...whom we
trust."
    The reference to Onesimus as belonging to the group of believers in
Colossae may be expressed as "who really belongs to your group" or "...to
you as a group of believers."

4.10   Aristarchus, who is in prison with me, sends you
greetings, and so does Mark, the cousin of Barnabas.
(You have already received instructions to welcome
Mark if he comes your way.)

With the exception of Joshua (verse 11), all individuals named in
verses 10-14 as sending greetings are also named in Philemon 23-24.
Aristarchus (see also Acts 19.29, 20.4, 27.2) is called Paul's "fellow
prisoner" (RSV). Some, like Moule and Beare, contend this is to be
understood metaphorically, that is, as a fellow prisoner of Christ's--so
NEB "Christ's captive like myself." Most, however (see Lohse), take it in
the literal sense.
    Languages differ considerably in the way in which they "send greetings."
For example, one may say "Aristarchus says he thinks of you," or "...wants
you to know he remembers you," or "...wishes to say, 'May you live well,'"
or "...says, May God be good to you."
    Mark (identified with the John Mark in Acts 12.12,25; 13.5,13; 15.37-
39; see also 2 Tim 4.11, 1 Peter 5.13) is identified as Barnabas' cousin
(KJV "nephew" is wrong), and reference is made to previous instructions
that had been sent to the Colossians to the effect that they should
welcome him if he visited them. There is no way of knowing in what form
the instructions had been sent.
    In view of the fact that no one knows precisely the form of the
instructions which had been sent to the believers in Colossae concerning
Mark, it may be best to simply say "you have been told to welcome Mark"
or "you have already received a letter in which you have been told to
welcome Mark," In a number of languages, "to welcome a person" may be
translated as "receive a person in your homes" or "to offer a person food
when he arrives."

4.11   Joshua, also called Justus, sends greetings too. These

three are the only Jewish converts who work with me
for the Kingdom of God, and they have been a great
help to me.

"Jesus" (RSV) is the graecized form of the Hebrew name Joshua (for
TEV's reason for using the Hebrew form, see TBT Oct. 1967, vol xviii,
page 168). It appears that he was better known by his Roman name, Justus,
rather than by his Hebrew name. Many Jews at that time had a Roman name
in addition to their Jewish name. Aristarchus, Mark, and Joshua are
identified as "men of the circumcision" (RSV), that is, Jews who had been
converted to the Christian faith; many translations have "Jewish Christians."
  Joshua, also called Justus may be translated as "Joshua who also
has the name of Justus" or "Joshua (people also call him Justus)."
  The only Jewish converts may be expressed as "the only Jews who
are now believers in Christ." Note, however, that the following conditional
clause, who work with me, further restricts the meaning of the only Jewish
converts.
  The Kingdom of God (compare 1.13) is used in the comprehensive sense
of the establishment of God's will on earth, for which Paul and his
companions were working. The phrase for the Kingdom of God may be expressed as "in order to cause the Kingdom of God to come" or, as in some
languages, "in order to make possible God's being King" or "...ruling
as King."
  Great help (TEV) or "comfort" (RSV) translates a word found only
here in the NT; "encouragement" is also a possible translation. They
have been a great help to me may be rendered as "they have helped me
very much."

4.12   Greetings from Epaphras, another member of your
            group and a servant of Christ Jesus. He always prays
            fervently for you, asking God to make you stand firm,
            as mature and fully convinced Christians, in complete
            obedience to God's will.

  Epaphras (1.7) is here, like Onesimus (verse 9), called "one of
yourselves" (RSV), that is, from the community or the church. Like Paul
(Rom 1.1, Phil 1.1) he is a servant of Christ Jesus. Greeting from Epaphras
may be better expressed in some languages as "Epaphras sends his greetings,"
or "Epaphras also wants to say that he remembers you," or "Epaphras also
wishes you well." The form which this greeting takes depends, of course,
upon the way in which greetings are generally expressed in writing. See
the discussion under verse 10.
  Another member of your group may be further specified as "another
person who belongs to your group of believers."
  A servant of Christ Jesus may be rendered as "one who works for
Christ Jesus."
  His manner of prayer, fervently (TEV) or "earnestly" (RSV) is expressed by the verb which in 1.29 is translated "struggle." It indicates
effort and intensity (JB "battling," Wey NIV "wrestling"). He always prays
fervently for you may be translated as "he always prays for you with all

his heart" or "his whole heart is in his prayers for you."

Epaphras' prayer is that God will make the Colossians stand firm, as mature and fully convinced Christians. The verb for stand firm is in the passive voice, and the prayer probably means that God is asked to make the Colossians stand firm. In a number of languages, the phrase stand firm may be best expressed as a negation of vacillation or change, for example, "he asks God to cause you not to change in your faith," or "...not to waver in your faith," or "...not to give up believing."

Mature translates the adjective teleios (see 1.28), and fully convinced Christians, represents the participle of plerophoreo, which could mean either "filled" (that is, "complete") or "convinced, assured" (Lohse prefers the former, Moule the latter). See the cognate noun plerophoria in 2.2. Brc has "firm in your faith, mature in your conviction."

Mature...Christians may be rendered as "those who are complete as Christians" or "those believers in whom nothing is lacking." Fully convinced Christians may then be rendered as "persons who are completely convinced in their belief in Christ," or "those who believe in Christ with all their hearts," or "those who have no doubts mixed with their faith."

4.13   I can personally testify to his hard work for you
        and for the people in Laodicea and Hierapolis.

This added praise of Epaphras makes it appear that he had been criticized for neglecting his work. Hard work translates polun ponon "much toil"; later manuscripts have zelon "zeal" (see KJV). I can personally testify to his hard work for you may be translated as "I myself am able to tell you about the way in which he has worked hard for you" or "I myself have seen how he has worked hard for you." Hard work for you may be rendered as "work hard in order to help you."

Hierapolis was about 20 kilometers northwest of Colossae. Hierapolis, Colossae, and Laodicea (see 2.1) were all in the Lycus Valley.

4.14   Luke, our dear doctor, and Demas send you their
        greetings.

Both Luke and Demas also appear in the letter to Philemon (verse 24). Luke is affectionately called dear doctor. Ancient tradition associates him with the Gospel of Luke and the Acts of the Apostles, but his name appears only here, Philemon 24, and 2 Tim 4.11. Demas appears again in 2 Tim 4.10.

The appositional construction Luke, our dear doctor, must often be expressed by a relative clause, for example, "Luke who is our dear doctor," or "Luke, our doctor, who is dear to us," or "...who is so much appreciated by us." Our in this context is obviously exclusive since Luke here functions as a doctor for Paul and his colleagues.

4.15   Give our best wishes to the brothers in Laodicea
        and to Nympha and the church that meets in her house.[f]

[f]Nympha...her house; some manuscripts have Nymphas...his house.

   With this verse Paul asks the Colossians to extend his greetings to the brothers in Laodicea, and also to Nympha and the church that meets in her house. It must be assumed that Nympha and the Christians associated with her are also in Laodicea, which would mean that besides the Christian group in Laodicea addressed as "the brothers," there is also this other Christian community. Beare suggests that Nympha and her group were possibly the church at Hierapolis or a rural congregation in the neighborhood.

   It is uncertain whether the person named is a woman, Nympha, or a man, "Nymphas." The decision rests on whether the pronoun to be read is "his" or "her"; the name itself in the Greek text can be accented either as a feminine or a masculine noun. Most commentators and translations prefer the feminine (Moule prefers the masculine). There is another variant reading, "their house," which Lightfoot prefers and explains as the house of Nymphas and his friends. For other examples of home-groups, see Rom 16.5 and 1 Cor 16.19 (Priscilla and Aquila); Philemon 2 (Philemon). Early Christians had no special houses of worship and met for worship in homes.

   Give our best wishes to the brothers in Laodicea may be rendered as "tell the brothers in Laodicea how much we wish the best for them."

   In this context the rendering of church must obviously refer to a group of believers. It cannot refer to a building. However, the church as a group of believers implies worshiping together, and therefore by redistributing some of the meaningful components of this term, it is possible to translate the church that meets in her house as "the believers who regularly worship God in her house."

4.16   After you read this letter, make sure that it is read also in the church at Laodicea. At the same time, you are to read the letter that the brothers in Laodicea will send you.

   Paul now instructs the Colossians to exchange letters with the church at Laodicea, so that the two letters, one to each church, are read in both churches. The context makes it almost certain that the letter that the brothers in Laodicea will send you is a letter that Paul is writing, or has written, to them; some, however, believe that it was a letter from the Laodiceans to Paul. Read means, in this context, reading aloud to the whole assembled group of Christians.

   A literal rendering of it is read also in the church at Laodicea might imply merely the building. It may, therefore, be better to say "it is read also to the believers at Laodicea" or "...to the group of believers at Laodicea."

   There has been much speculation about this letter of Paul to the Laodiceans. Some have thought it is what is now called Ephesians, or Philemon, or even Hebrews. Already by the end of the fourth century there was a fabricated "Letter to the Laodiceans," of which only Latin copies survive, but which was originally written in Greek. It was included in many copies of the Latin Bible from the sixth century to the fifteenth century. It is a mindless collection of Pauline phrases, which Lightfoot calls "quite harmless, so far as falsity and stupidity combined can ever be regarded as harmless."[12] The most likely explanation is that the letter Paul refers to here was lost or destroyed.

A literal translation of at the same time might suggest simultaneous reading of two letters. A more accurate and satisfactory rendering may be "similarly, you are to read the letter..." or "in the same way you are to read the letter..."

In rendering the letter that the brothers in Laodicea will send you, it is important to avoid the implication that this is a letter written by the fellow believers in Laodicea. The letter was written by Paul and sent to the believers in Laodicea who are to send it on to the believers in Colossae.

4.17   And tell Archippus, "Be sure to finish the task you
         were given in the Lord's service."

The precise meaning of the message to Archippus (who appears also in Philemon 2 as one of the recipients of that letter) is impossible to determine. There are various interpretations about the task or "ministry" (Greek diakonia) that Archippus was to complete, but no one can be dogmatic. It appears to be some specific matter, not Archippus' ministry as a Christian.

The sequence of two imperative expressions, one consisting of direct discourse included within another imperative, may be quite difficult to understand, especially when the passage is read aloud. Those who hear it read may not understand at first that the direct discourse applies simply to Archippus rather than to the believers in Colossae. Therefore, it may be better, in this instance, to use indirect discourse, for example, "tell Archippus that he must finish the task which he was given in the service of the Lord" or "...as one who is to help the Lord."

4.18   With my own hand I write this: Greetings from Paul.
         Do not forget my chains!
         May God's grace be with you.

Thus far Paul had dictated the letter, but he himself writes the final greeting (see also 1 Cor 16.21, Gal 6.11, 2 Thes 3.17). He calls upon them to remember that he is in prison (see 4.3). The closing salutation, as in all Pauline letters, prays that God's grace (or, in most of them, the grace of Jesus Christ) be with them. For grace see 1.2.

The statement with my own hand I write this may be confusing since the pronoun this so frequently refers back to something which as been previously said. The relationship to what follows may be made quite clear by saying "I'm writing the following words with my own hand." It may even be appropriate to introduce greetings from Paul as a type of indirect discourse, for example, "with my own hand I am writing these greetings to you."

Do not forget my chains may be effectively expressed as "do not forget that I am in jail."

May God's grace be with you may be expressed as "may God be kind to you" or "may God show his goodness to you." Such a request must, however, be expressed in a number of languages in the form of a prayer, for example, "I pray that God will be gracious to you."

TRANSLATING PHILEMON

Paul's letter to Philemon is the most personal of all his letters. It is written on behalf of Onesimus, a slave who had fled from his master Philemon and had somehow become Paul's friend and convert to the Christian faith while Paul was in prison (verse 10). Paul is returning Onesimus to his master, and the letter is written to intercede with Philemon, who had been converted to the Christian faith by Paul (verse 10), to receive Onesimus back as a Christian brother (verses 15-17). It should be remembered that at that time a runaway slave, when caught, could be put to death by his master.

This letter is closely related to Paul's letter to the Colossians. Assuming that Colossians is by Paul (which some scholars deny), the letter to Philemon was written at the same time and from the same place as the letter to the Christians at Colossae (see Introduction to Colossians).

In Colossians 4.9, Onesimus is said to be from Colossae; as a consequence, it must be assumed that Philemon, Apphia, Archippus, and the church that meets in Philemon's house are all also in Colossae, but this is not explicitly said in the letter to Philemon.

Paul is in prison (verses 1,10,23); Timothy is named as a fellow writer (verse 1); and with Paul are Epaphras, Mark, Aristarchus, Demas, and Luke (verses 23-24). He hopes to be set free from prison before long and to go visit Philemon and the others (verse 22).

Outline of Contents

A. Salutation (1-3)

B. Philemon's Love and Faith (4-7)

C. A Request on Behalf of Onesimus (8-22)

D. Final Greetings and Benediction (23-25)

TEV	(1.1-3)	RSV

1 From Paul, a prisoner for the sake of Christ Jesus, and from our brother Timothy-- To our friend and fellow worker Philemon, 2 and the church that meets in your house, and our sister Apphia, and our fellow soldier Archippus:

3 May God our Father and the Lord Jesus Christ give you grace and peace.

1 Paul, a prisoner for Christ Jesus, and Timothy our brother, To Philemon our beloved fellow worker 2 and Apphia our sister and Archippus our fellow soldier, and the church in your house:

3 Grace to you and peace from God our Father and the Lord Jesus Christ.

The title for the book of Philemon may have several different forms. In some biblical texts it is known simply as "Philemon," but this can be quite misleading, since it might suggest that the book is about Philemon. Other texts have the title as "A Letter to Philemon." This is better, but in most instances a somewhat fuller title, namely "Paul's Letter to Philemon," is preferable. For a running head at the top of the page (if the letter goes on for more than one page) the name "Philemon" is generally employed.

In most instances no introductory section heading is employed for a "salutation." It would, of course, be possible to say "Paul addresses Philemon," but in general it seems best to omit an initial section heading.

The opening of the letter is standard, consisting of identifying the writer, or writers (verse 1a), the recipients (verses 1b-2), and Christian greetings (verse 3).

The structure of the salutation must be rather extensively changed in some languages in order to make it fully intelligible. These modifications will be dealt with in connection with the contents of verses 1-3.

1.1-2   From Paul, a prisoner for the sake of Christ
             Jesus, and from our brother, Timothy--
             To our friend and fellow worker Philemon, 2
             and the church that meets in your house, and our
             sister Apphia, and our fellow soldier Archippus:

In a number of languages, it is not possible to speak of oneself in the third person, and therefore it may be necessary to employ a first person pronoun, together with the name "Paul"; hence, "from me, Paul" or "I Paul write to..."

Paul begins this letter by identifying himself as a prisoner for the sake of Christ Jesus (also verse 9), which means he was in jail because of his Christian work (verses 10,13), or, in a figurative sense, that he was "a prisoner of Christ Jesus," that is, he was held captive by him. The latter is possible, but not very probable, since Paul usually identifies himself as an apostle of Christ (Rom 1.1, 1 Cor 1.1, 2 Cor

1.1, Gal 1.1, Eph 1.1, Col 1.1) or as a slave of Christ (Rom 1.1, Phil
1.1). The phrase a prisoner for the sake of Christ Jesus must often be
made into an entire clause, for example, "I am now in prison for the
sake of Christ Jesus."

A literal rendering of the phrase for the sake of Christ Jesus
might be understood in the sense of Paul being a prisoner in order to
advance the cause of Christ Jesus, but what is meant is that he became
a prisoner because of what he had already done to advance the cause of
Christ Jesus. Therefore, it may be necessary to introduce a more explicit
statement concerning the reasons for Paul being in prison, for example,
"I am in prison because of what I have done for the sake of Christ Jesus"
or "...to serve Christ Jesus."

Brother is used of Timothy in the Christian sense of a fellow believer in Christ. Paul associates Timothy with himself in writing the
letter, but in the letter itself Paul speaks for himself alone. Since
the role of Timothy in the sending of this letter is secondary, it may
be important to indicate this fact by translating "our brother Timothy
joins me in sending greetings" or "...in sending this letter." In this
way one may indicate that Paul is the principal author of the letter.

In a number of languages, it is impossible to use a term meaning
literally "brother," since this would refer only to an individual who is
a member of the same family. Therefore, "fellow believer" may be the most
satisfactory equivalent. In certain instances, this relationship of Timothy to the Christian faith can only be expressed by a relative clause,
"who also believes in Christ Jesus" or "...has put his trust in Christ
Jesus."

Philemon is addressed as our friend and fellow worker (TEV) or "our
beloved fellow worker" (RSV). Either translation of the phrase is possible.

It may be necessary to introduce a second person singular pronoun
in order to identify the relationship of Paul to Philemon, for example,
"to you, Philemon, our friend and fellow worker."

Fellow worker must not, however, be translated in such a way as to
suggest that Paul and Philemon were both day laborers. What is meant is
that Philemon also helped in advancing the cause of Christ. Therefore,
one may translate "one who works with us to help Christ," or "...to serve
Christ," or "...to make Christ known."

And the church that meets in your house (on which see Col 4.15) is
placed by TEV (also SpCL FrCL BrCL) immediately following Philemon's
name in order to make it clear that your refers to Philemon and not to
Archippus, as might be understood when placed at the end of verse 2. Although some believe that Archippus is the main addressee of the letter,
the vast majority hold that the first-named of the three persons is the
main recipient of the letter, and that the person addressed by the second person singular pronoun in all the requests in verses 4-23 is in
fact Philemon, even though his name as such does not appear. If it is
judged better to keep the church in your house at the end of verse 2, in
order to avoid misunderstanding, it might be well to say, as do TC GeCL
TNT, "in Philemon's house."

In the same way that Philemon must be identified in some languages
with a second person singular pronoun, it may also be necessary to use

[114]

a similar pronoun in speaking of the church, for example, "and to you who are members of the church that meets in the house of Philemon." On the other hand, the letter is so predominantly addressed to Philemon that it may be misleading to suggest that the church that met in Philemon's house, Apphia, and Archippus are all on the same level as recipients of the letter. Therefore, one may be obliged to translate as follows, "to you, Philemon, our friend and fellow worker, and will you extend greetings to the church that meets in your house and to our sister Apphia and to our fellow soldier Archippus."

Apphia is called our sister, a phrase used also in the Christian sense of a fellow believer. There is no way of determining what was the relation between her, Philemon, and Archippus. Some may think that she was Philemon's wife, which is quite possible, and that Archippus was their son; but all of this is purely conjectural. Some later manuscripts add the adjective "beloved" to Apphia (see KJV).

A literal rendering of our sister Apphia can be misleading, not only because "sister" might be taken in the literal sense, but also because the possessive pronoun "our" might suggest some kind of possessive relationship. To avoid this misunderstanding, one may translate, for example, "Apphia, who also believes in Christ Jesus even as we do."

Archippus is addressed as our fellow soldier, in a figurative sense of one who "fights" for the Christian cause (used also in Phil 2.25 of Epaphroditus). A literal rendering of soldier can be misleading. In some instances this metaphorical or figurative meaning may be identified satisfactorily as a simile, for example, "who is like a soldier." The essential meaning may also be supplied by a non-figurative expression, for example, "who strives so hard to serve" or "who faces so much opposition in serving." The phrase our fellow may be expressed as "even as we do" or "who together with us."

1.3   May God our Father and the Lord Jesus Christ
          give you grace and peace.

Again we find the standard Pauline greeting, in which he prays that grace and peace may be given them by God our Father (as in Col 1.2). Here Paul adds further and the Lord Jesus Christ (as in Rom 1.7, 1 Cor 1.3, 2 Cor 1.2, Gal 1.3, Phil 1.2). The letter is not a purely personal one (you is plural), even though the request on Onesimus' behalf is made to the one person, Philemon. The matter, while essentially Philemon's responsibility, is also of concern to the others.

The third person request May God our Father and the Lord Jesus Christ give you grace and peace must be introduced in a number of languages by a statement suggesting prayer or petition, for example, "I pray that God our father..."

The appositional construction God our Father may be rendered in some languages as a noun followed by a relative clause, for example, "God who is our Father." In initial translations in a language, it is sometimes important to indicate that "our Father" is to be understood in a figurative sense, for example, "God who is like our father" or "God who is like a father to us."

In a number of languages, <u>Lord</u> must be identified in relationship to those to whom he is Lord. Therefore, one must say "our Lord" or "he who is Lord over us."

<u>Give you grace</u> is rendered in a number of languages as "show you kindness" or "show you goodness from his heart," thus suggesting that the goodness is nothing which is deserved by the recipients but something which comes as the result of unmerited favor.

<u>Peace</u> is not to be understood in this context as absence of war. Here the focus is more upon the psychological and spiritual aspects of peace, sometimes rendered in rather figurative language, for example, "may God our Father and the Lord Jesus Christ cause you...to sit down in your hearts" or "...to rest your livers."

TEV	(1.4-7)	RSV

PHILEMON'S LOVE AND FAITH

TEV	RSV
4 Brother Philemon, every time I pray, I mention you and give thanks to my God. 5 For I hear of your love for all of God's people and the faith you have in the Lord Jesus. 6 My prayer is that our fellowship with you as believers will bring about a deeper understanding of every blessing which we have in our life in union with Christ. 7 Your love, dear brother, has brought me great joy and much encouragement! You have cheered the hearts of all of God's people.	4 I thank my God always when I remember you in my prayers, 5 because I hear of your love and of the faith which you have toward the Lord Jesus and all the saints 6 and I pray that the sharing of your faith may promote the knowledge of all the good that is ours in Christ. 7 For I have derived much joy and comfort from your love, my brother, because the hearts of the saints have been refreshed through you.

In a prayer of thanksgiving (verse 4), Paul (1) praises Philemon's love and faith (verse 5), (2) prays that the fellowship which exists between Paul and Philemon may result in a greater understanding of the blessings which are theirs as Christians (verse 6), and (3) expresses gratitude for what Philemon's love has meant to him and other Christians (verse 7).

The section heading <u>Philemon's Love and Faith</u> must often be expanded, particularly if the concepts of <u>Love</u> and <u>Faith</u> must be expressed as verbs, for example, "how Philemon loves God's people and trusts the Lord Jesus."

1.4   Brother Philemon, every time I pray, I mention you and give thanks to my God.

TEV has made clear that Paul is addressing only one person, namely Philemon (see also FrCL GeCL TNT Phps). The name <u>Philemon</u> alone would in

English be too distant, so brother is used (see verse 7). In certain
instances Brother Philemon may be expressed as "my dear Philemon" or
"Philemon, my friend." Frequently, however, there is some standard expression in languages to identify fellow Christians, and this would be
an appropriate expression in this context, but it should carry the connotation of friendship and intimacy. In some languages an expression
such as "relative" is used, and in other cases "fellow clansman."

TEV has rearranged the three items in Paul's statement: (1) he
prays, (2) he mentions Philemon, and (3) he thanks God. The adverb "always" (RSV) goes with I mention you, and the sense of "when I pray, I
always mention you" is represented by every time I pray I mention you.

I mention you (also Mft Gpd NEB Brc TOB JB) is one way of understanding the Greek phrase (compare Lightfoot, Moule); RSV "I remember
you" (also TNT NIV FrCL GeCL SpCL) is another way. The former seems more
appropriate as a deliberate act, not a chance happening. A literal translation such as "I remember you" might suggest in some languages that
Paul had forgotten about Philemon. The meaning of the Greek term rendered
"remember" in RSV really means in this context, "to constantly bear in
mind." One can, therefore, translate "whenever I pray, I bear you in
mind" or "...I constantly think of you."

Paul, like the OT psalmists (for example, Psa 3.7, 5.2, 22.2, 25.2),
uses my God to emphasize the intensity of his personal relation with God.
In a number of languages, one cannot say "my God," since this would
suggest that the individual in question possesses God. The correct rendering of this phrase may, therefore, be "the God whom I worship." On
the other hand, an emphatic form of "I" might suggest "the God whom I
worship but you do not," in which case an inclusive form of "we" could
be employed for this particular context.

I give thanks: see Col 1.3.

In a number of languages, I...give thanks to my God must be translated in such a way as to indicate the content of the thanks, for example, "I give thanks to my God because of you." Often, however, the expression I...give thanks must be restructured as direct discourse, since
it implies some kind of utterance, for example, "I say to my God, 'I am
thankful for Philemon.'" However, this may be expressed somewhat more
satisfactorily as indirect discourse, for example, "I say to my God that
I am thankful to you." In some instances "thankfulness" can only be expressed in terms of an emotion of happiness, for example, "I am happy
because of you." Thankfulness can be most satisfactorily expressed in
some languages as a causative of an emotion, for example, "because you
cause my heart to be glad."

1.5   For I hear of your love for all of God's people
             and the faith you have in the Lord Jesus.

Paul says that two things he has heard make him thank God for
Philemon: Philemon's love for all of God's people and his faith in the
Lord Jesus. The Greek text employs a literary figure known as chiasmus
(see Lightfoot, Moule), in which the order of the elements in two parallel phrases is a-b-b-a: love-faith-Lord Jesus-saints. TEV (also FrCL

GeCL Brc BrCL) has abandoned the figure, since a literal reproduction of it (as in RSV JB NAB) leads to misunderstanding. The contents of the verse are identical with that of Col 1.4. Some take pistis here in the sense of "faithfulness, loyalty," because of the preposition pros "to, toward" and the use of "the Lord" as the one to whom the pistis is directed. But the same preposition is used in 1 Thes 1.8, and the usual meaning of "faith," in Paul's letters, that is, trust in Christ, is most probably the one intended here.

Since what Paul heard was actually a report of Philemon's love for God's people, it may be important to make this relationship explicit, for example, "I have heard people speak about your love for all of God's people " or even "people have told me how much you love all of God's people." If this must be expressed in direct discourse, one may say "people have told me,'Philemon loves all of God's people.'"

In translating the term love, it is important to avoid connotations of sexual interest and of "desire" in the sense of "desiring to possess" or "wanting to control." A more satisfactory equivalent in some languages is "how you take care of all of God's people" or "how you are so concerned for all of God's people." The emphasis is upon the manner in which Philemon has a desire to help God's people rather than his emotional attachment to God's people.

The faith you have in the Lord Jesus may be expressed as "the way in which you trust the Lord Jesus" or "...our Lord Jesus."

1.6   My prayer is that our fellowship with you as be-
       lievers will bring about a deeper understanding
       of every blessing which we have in our life in
       union with Christ.

In place of the noun phrase My prayer, one may often more conveniently use a verb expression "I pray that..."

As Moule says, "this is notoriously the most obscure verse in this letter."[13] Paul here gives the content of his petition. The first phrase in Greek is literally "that the fellowship of your faith," and it is variously understood: (1) NEB "your fellowship with us in our common faith" (also Brc and C.H.Dodd); (2) NAB "your sharing of the faith with others"; (3) FrCL "the fellowship which binds you to us by means of the faith"; (4) BrCL "the Christian fellowship that binds you to us"; (5) GeCL "the faith in which you share" (also Lohse). TEV takes koinōnia to be the fellowship which is based on faith; but other interpretations are just as possible, as demonstrated by the wide variety exhibited. Lightfoot takes koinōnia here to have the sense it sometimes has of "kindly deeds of charity, which spring from your faith" (see Phil 1.5 for this meaning of the word).

The TEV rendering our fellowship with you as believers may be rendered as "how as believers we are one with you" or "how we are joined together with you as believers" or "...as those who trust in Christ." The NEB rendering "your fellowship with us in our common faith" may be rendered as "how you join with us in the trust which we all have in Christ." If "faith" is to be understood as the means of such fellowship as in the FrCL, then one may say "the way in which you are bound to us because of our common trust in Christ" or "the way in which you become

one together with us because of the way in which we all trust Christ."
Will bring about a deeper understanding: it is not clear in whom
this deeper understanding is to be effected, whether it is Philemon in
particular, or Philemon and all others who are involved, including Paul
and his companions. For the latter, TNT has "we may all," and Brc "us";
for the former, BJ JB TC GeCL NIV have "you." It may be that Paul has
Philemon particularly in mind, but does not want to say so explicitly.

This expression may be rendered as a causative, for example, "will
cause us all to understand better" or "...understand more fully." If
those who are to have a more adequate understanding is to be expressed
in somewhat more general terms, it is, of course, possible to say "will
cause all believers to understand better."

Bring about translates energēs genētai "may become effective, pro-
ductive."

For deeper understanding, a translation of epignōsis, see Col 1.9.

Every blessing (TEV) or "all the good" (RSV) are both possible ways
of translating the Greek. In any case, Paul is not thinking of material
"good things," but of spiritual benefits. Every blessing must often be
expressed as a clause, "all that God has done" or "all the good that
comes from God."

"Ours" (RSV) is the reading preferred by modern commentators and
translators, but the variant reading "yours" has wide and excellent
support (see KJV). We have in our life includes all Christians and is
not restricted to Paul and his group.

In our life in union with Christ (similarly TNT NEB Phps FrCL BrCL)
translates the Greek "into (eis) Christ." There are other ways of translating this, depending on how the phrase is made to relate to the preceding words. BJ TOB JB "the good things we are able to do for Christ";
NEBmg "all the blessings that bring us to Christ"; Brc "and so may lead
us nearer and nearer to Christ"; Lohse (also Vincent) "for the glory of
Christ"; Lightfoot "leading to Christ." It must be recognized that eis
Christon is an unusual phrase and probably should not be taken as simply
the equivalent of en Christō, "(our life) in union with Christ." The
preposition eis generally denotes movement, progress, direction; so something like "leading to Christ" may well be the most defensible rendering
of this admittedly obscure phrase.

If one follows the rendering of the TEV, every blessing which we
have in our life in union with Christ, it is possible to translate as
"every blessing which we have received (from God) as a result of our
union with Christ," or "all that is good which we have as we live joined
with Christ," or "...in close fellowship with Christ." Note, however, the
other possible interpretations, for example, as in BJ TOB JB, "all the
good that we are able to do in order to serve Christ."

1.7   Your love, dear brother, has brought me great joy
             and much encouragement! You have cheered the hearts
             of all of God's people.

The phrase dear brother is a rendering of what in Greek is literally
"brother" in a form of direct address, but in this context such a vocative
expression suggests more than "brother" alone would, and therefore the

addition of "dear" is justified in order to suggest the friendship which Paul is emphasizing. Dear brother may be rendered as "my dear fellow believer" or, as in some languages, "my dear friend."

The key words are love (see verse 5), joy (see Col 1.11), and encouragement (TEV) or "comfort" (RSV); see the cognate verb parakaleō in Col 2.2, 4.8. TEV has transformed the sentence from the passive (RSV "I have derived...from your love") to an active (your love...has brought me), as being more appropriate in English in this context.

Your love...has brought me great joy may be restructured as "because of your love, I have great joy," or "...I rejoice very much," or "...I am exceedingly happy." It is important in this context to indicate clearly that your love refers to Philemon's love for fellow believers and the way in which he obviously manifests that concern in helping them.

Has brought me...much encouragement may be expressed as "has caused me to take heart" or "...to have courage again." This may be expressed metaphorically in some languages as "to cause my heart to be strong again."

Some translations, like RSV, join the two statements with "because," taking the second one as the reason for the first one. Other translations, like TEV, take the two as essentially separate statements.

Cheered the hearts represents the Greek "the hearts have been refreshed." The verb anapauō (also verse 20) means "to revive, refresh." Hearts represents the Greek "the bowels," which is a biblical way of speaking of the emotions, the inner feelings (also verses 12,20).

You have cheered the hearts of all of God's people may be expressed as "you have caused all of God's people to be happy" or, expressed metaphorically, "...have caused the hearts of all of God's people to sing" or "...to dance."

For God's people see Col 1.2.

TEV	(1.8-22)	RSV

A REQUEST FOR ONESIMUS

8 For this reason I could be bold enough, as your brother in Christ, to order you to do what should be done. 9 But because I love you, I make a request instead. I do this even though I am Paul, the ambassador of Christ Jesus, and at present also a prisoner for his sake.[a] 10 So I make a request to you on behalf of Onesimus, who is my own son in Christ; for while in prison I have become his spiritual father. 11 At one time he was of no use to you, but now he is useful both to you and to me.

8 Accordingly, though I am bold enough in Christ to command you to do what is required, 9 yet for love's sake I prefer to appeal to you--I, Paul, an ambassador[a] and now a prisoner also for Christ Jesus-- 10 I appeal to you for my child, Onesimus, whose father I have become in my imprisonment. 11 (Formerly he was useless to you but now he is indeed useful[b] to you and to me.) 12 I am sending him back to you, sending my very heart. 13 I would have been glad to keep him with me, in order that he might serve me on your behalf during my imprisonment for the gospel; 14 but

12 I am sending him back to you now, and with him goes my heart. 13 I would like to keep him here with me, while I am in prison for the gospel's sake, so that he could help me in your place. 14 However, I do not want to force you to help me; rather, I would like for you to do it of your own free will. So I will not do anything unless you agree.

15 It may be that Onesimus was away from you for a short time so that you might have him back for all time. 16 And now he is not just a slave, but much more than a slave: he is a dear brother in Christ. How much he means to me! And how much more he will mean to you, both as a slave and as a brother in the Lord!

17 So, if you think of me as your partner, welcome him back just as you would welcome me. 18 If he has done you any wrong or owes you anything, charge it to my account. 19 Here, I will write this with my own hand: I, Paul, will pay you back. (I should not have to re-mind you, of course, that you owe your very self to me.) 20 So, my brother, please do me this favor for the Lord's sake; as a brother in Christ, cheer me up!

21 I am sure, as I write this, that you will do what I ask--in fact I know that you will do even more. 22 At the same time, get a room ready for me, be-cause I hope that God will an-swer the prayers of all of you and give me back to you.

^athe ambassador of Christ Jesus, and at present also a prisoner for his sake; or an old man, and at present a prisoner for the sake of Christ Jesus.

I preferred to do nothing without your consent in order that your goodness might not be by compulsion but of your own free will.

15 Perhaps this is why he was parted from you for a while, that you might have him back for ever, 16 no longer as a slave but more than a slave, as a beloved brother, especially to me but how much more to you, both in the flesh and in the Lord. 17 So if you consider me your partner, receive him as you would receive me. 18 If he has wronged you at all, or owes you anything, charge that to my account. 19 I, Paul, write this with my own hand, I will repay it--to say nothing of your owing me even your own self. 20 Yes, brother, I want some benefit from you in the Lord. Refresh my heart in Christ.

21 Confident of your obedience, I write to you, knowing that you will do even more than I say. 22 At the same time, prepare a guest room for me, for I am hoping through your prayers to be granted to you.

^aOr an old man

^bThe name Onesimus means useful or (verse 20) beneficial

[121]

The body of the letter is taken up with Paul's request to Philemon on the behalf of Onesimus, which is done with extraordinary tact and consideration. Notwithstanding his authority as an apostle and his present circumstances as a prisoner, Paul does not command but pleads on behalf of Onesimus (verses 8-9), whose past and present situation he recounts (verses 10-11). Paul is returning Onesimus to Philemon, even though he would have liked to keep him in order that he might help Paul (verses 12-13); but Paul will not do anything without Philemon's consent (verse 14). And with a delicacy unmatched in his other letters, Paul suggests that Philemon should see in Onesimus' flight the result of divine providence, transforming the relationship between master and slave (verses 15-16). Paul asks Philemon to receive Onesimus back (verse 17), promises personally to make good any loss Philemon may have suffered (verses 18-19), and concludes with an eloquent plea, based on Christian motives (verse 20). He expresses confidence that Philemon will comply with his request (verse 21), and couples that with the additional request that Philemon be ready to receive him, because he hopes to be with them before long (verse 22).

The section heading A Request For Onesimus may be made somewhat more explicit as "Paul makes a request for Onesimus" or "Paul asks Philemon to be kind to Onesimus."

1.8   For this reason I could be bold enough, as
        your brother in Christ, to order you to do what
        should be done.

In Greek this verse is concessive in force ("even though I could ..."), which carries on into verse 9 ("instead, I ask you..."). This element is picked up and repeated in verse 10 ("I ask you..."). For greater ease of understanding, most translations break up into simpler sentences this complex sentence, which goes without a major break until the end of verse 12.

For this reason refers back to the contents of the preceding section (verses 4-7) and specifically to Philemon's well-known love for his fellow Christians (verses 5,7). A literal rendering of for this reason may not be sufficient to show the relationship between the body of the letter and the introductory section. Therefore, it may be advisable to mark the relationship somewhat more explicitly, for example, "because of the way in which you love God's people" or "...show concern for God's people."

I could be bold enough. The noun parrēsia means primarily "freedom in speech," and by extension "boldness, confidence" in attitude. Here it clearly implies that Paul has the right, the authority, to command Philemon, but refrains from using it. Since Paul does not order Philemon to do what he should, it may be necessary to make this somewhat more explicit, for example, "I could be bold enough, but I will not be." This may be combined effectively with the clause, to order you to do what should be done: "I could tell you with strong words what should be done, but I will not."

As your brother in Christ translates the Greek en Christō. Here

more than "as a Christian" seems to be implied; it appears to involve
not just Paul's own status as a Christian (so Gpd), but the relationship
between him and Philemon. So Brc "our relationship as Christians" (see
TNT). Others take it in the sense, "although the right has been given me
by Christ" (Wey FrCL Phps); SpCL has "as an apostle of Christ"; GeCL has
"by referring to Christ." As your brother in Christ may be rendered
"as one who also trusts in Christ," or "as one who trusts in Christ even
as you do," or "as one who is a follower of Christ even as you are."

To order translates epitassō, found only here in Paul's letters;
it implies a superiority in rank. A verb such as epitassō in the meaning
of "to order" or "to command" must be rendered in a number of languages
as a verb introducing direct discourse, for example, "to order you,'This
is what you must do.'"

What should be done: for a similar use of the verb anēkō see Col
3.18. Paul does not spell out specifically what Philemon should do, but
by indirection and implication he makes it clear enough. Philemon should
receive Onesimus as a Christian brother and then set him free so that he
can return to Paul to help him in his work (verse 13-14).

1.9   But because I love you, I make a request in-
       stead. I do this even though I am Paul, the
       ambassador of Christ Jesus, and at the present
       also a prisoner for his sake.[a]

       [a]the ambassador of Christ Jesus, and at present
       also a prisoner for his sake; or an old man, and
       at present a prisoner for the sake of Christ Jesus.

Because I love you represents the Greek "on account of love," which
might be rendered impersonally "on the basis of (Christian) love," or
mutually, "because we love one another" (Brc). The rendering of love in
this context should suggest friendship and sincere appreciation.

I make a request translates parakaleō (also verse 10), here with
the meaning of "to plead, appeal," perhaps "to beg a favor." An appeal
is often expressed figuratively, for example, "I ask you with my heart
exposed" or "I ask you from my abdomen."

What follows in the verse comes as a concessive clause, even though
I am, which implies that what Paul is gives him the right to do otherwise than make a request. The concessive clause I do this even though...
may be restructured in some languages as "I could do it differently, for
I am..."

Ambassador translates the Greek presbutēs, which is usually "an
old man" (see Luke 1.18, Titus 2.2; "old women" in Titus 2.3). But this
word sometimes appears as a variant spelling of presbeutēs, and on this
basis TEV RSV NAB BrCL NEB TNT Brc Gpd TC and others take it here to
mean ambassador, which seems much more appropriate in the context (so
Lightfoot, Moule). (The noun presbeutēs does not appear in the NT, but
the cognate verb presbeuō is used in 2 Cor 5.20, Eph 6.20.) Others (Vincent, Lohse) think "an old man" is meant, and that is how it is translated in JB GeCL TOB FrCL SpCL NIV Mft Phps. It is impossible to decide

precisely how old Paul would be; according to the sixth-century B.C. Greek physician Hippocrates, this word applied to an individual between 49 and 56.

Ambassador may be rendered as "one who represents" or "one who carries a message on behalf of" or "one who travels in order to speak for."

A prisoner for his sake: see verse 1.

1.10   So I make a request to you on behalf of Onesimus,
           who is my own son in Christ; for while in prison
           I have become his spiritual father.

Again Paul repeats I make a request; it is on behalf of Onesimus, whom he calls "my child" (RSV). In order to make clear that this is a spiritual relationship, TEV has my own son in Christ and spiritual father (compare Brc "I became his father in the faith"). While Paul was in prison, he was able to lead Onesimus to accept the Christian faith. In 1 Cor 4.15, Paul also uses the figure of "begetting" people as Christian converts.

I make a request is equivalent in some languages to "I ask you please."

One behalf of Onesimus may be expressed in some instances as "concerning Onesimus," but it is better to try to introduce Onesimus as the one who is going to benefit from such a request; therefore, "I ask you as a help to Onesimus."

The figurative expression in the clause who is my own son must be restructured as a simile in some languages, for example, "who is, as it were, my own son" or "who has become, so to speak, my own son." The phrase in Christ may then be combined as "who as now a fellow believer in Christ is, as it were, my own son."

I have become his spiritual father must also be expressed in some languages as a simile, for example, "I have become, so to speak, his father." What is expressed in the TEV as spiritual also suggests the figurative meaning of "father," but it is difficult in a number of languages to find a ready equivalent of spiritual. Therefore, the introduction of an expression such as "so to speak" or "as it were" is perhaps the best way of qualifying this significant metaphor. In some cases, one may say "I have become his father in that he is now a part of the family of believers," but such an expression would seem to be too expanded.

On the basis of the relation of the accusative form of Onesimus in Greek to the verb "I begot," John Knox infers that the name Onesimus is the slave's Christian name, given him by Paul.[14]

1.11   At one time he was of no use to you, but now he
           is useful both to you and to me.

In this verse there is an allusion to the name Onesimus, which means "profitable, beneficial." (The noun onēsis "profit" comes from the verb oninēmi "to profit, benefit," which appears in verse 20.) The adjective "useless" (RSV) occurs only here in the NT; "useful" appears also in 2 Tim 2.21, 4.11. Paul is referring to the change in Onesimus from what he was formerly. Though not conclusive, verse 18 implies that Onesimus had stolen some valuables when he ran away from Philemon; and a slave who ran away was, by definition, quite useless. The two adjectives have the broadest meaning and are not to be restricted only to financial loss or profit.

The temporal phrase at one time may be best expressed in many instances as "formerly" or "in the past." At one time does not mean "on one occasion."

He was of no use to you may be expressed as "he did you no good," or "he was no help to you," or "he did not in any way help you." Similarly, the last part of this verse may be expressed as "but now he helps both you and me" or "...can be helpful to both you and me."

There is practically no way in which the pun on the meaning of the name Onesimus can be reproduced in translation, and therefore it may be useful to introduce a marginal note at this point to indicate the play on the meaning of the name Onesimus.

Both to you and to me may be expressed in a more polite and appropriate form in some languages as "not only to you but also to me."

1.12   I am sending him back to you now, and with him
              goes my heart.

I am sending...back represents the epistolary aorist (see Col 4.8). What follows in Greek, "that is, my own heart," is in apposition to "him." What Paul means is that his love, concern, most intimate feelings are tied up with Onesimus' future, and in returning him to Philemon, Paul is sending his own deepest interests. It is as though Paul himself were going to Philemon.

In selecting a verb to translate sending, it is important to employ a term which is applicable to individuals and not merely to objects. An appropriate translation of I am sending him back to you now must often be rendered as a causative, for example, "I am now causing him to go back to you," or "...to travel back to you," or "...to return to you."

The clause and with him goes my heart is an excellent idiomatic rendering of the underlying Greek text, but it is rare that such an expression can be translated literally into other languages. A more appropriate equivalent may be "he is one who is very dear to me" or "I love him very much."

This verse was much altered by copyists; for a late resultant text, see KJV.

The Greek for heart here is the same as in verse 7.

1.13   I would like to keep him here with me, while I
              am in prison for the gospel's sake, so that he
              could help me in your place.

Paul, with great diffidence, approaches the request he is about to make. I would like to keep him, or perhaps better in English, "I would have liked to keep him," indicates his personal preference in the matter, which he is forgoing in view of the fact that by right the decision about

Onesimus' future belongs to Philemon, not to Paul. (For similar use of eboulomēn see Acts 25.22.)

I would like to keep him here with me suggests something that Paul would not do, and therefore it may be necessary to make this fact explicit, for example, "I would like to keep him here with me but I will not do so." To keep him here with me may be rendered as a causative, for example, "I would like to cause him to remain with me."

There is a rather awkward relationship between clauses in verse 13, for persons could understand the purpose clause so that he could help me in your place as being related to while I am in prison for the gospel's sake. Obviously, however, the clause so that he could help me in your place goes with I would like to keep him here with me. It may, therefore, be preferable to place the temporal clause at the beginning of verse 13, for example, "while I am in prison for the gospel's sake, I would like to keep him here with me so that he can help me in your place."

He could help (TEV) or "he might serve" (RSV) translates the subjunctive of the verb diakoneō. The general meaning "to help" is preferable, since Paul speaks of Onesimus' doing this in Philemon's place; "serve" might be understood to refer to rather menial or degrading work in prison.

In your place: Paul is saying that Onesimus would be doing what Philemon would have been glad to do (see especially Brc). It is frequently necessary to make the relationships indicated in the phrase in your place somewhat more specific. For example, the last clause of verse 13 may be rendered as "so that he could help me by doing what you would do if you were here."

In prison for the gospel's sake: Paul does not specify the occasion of being arrested and jailed because of his activities as an apostle. The words may be translated as "in prison because of having announced the good news," or "...because I preached the good news," or "because of my faithfulness to the good news."

1.14   However, I do not want to force you to help me;
            rather, I would like for you to do it of your
            free will. So I will not do anything unless you
            agree.

In an attempt to make the flow of thought easier to assimilate, TEV has restructured considerably the contents of the verse; RSV follows closely the form of the Greek.

To force you (TEV) represents the Greek kata anagkēn (which in RSV appears as "by compulsion"). The word represents the outward pressure or force that is laid on someone, under which he is forced to act in a certain way. "Under duress" would be a modern equivalent of the phrase. I do not want to force you to help me may be expressed as "I do not want you to help me because you think you must do so" or "...because I make you help me."

To help me represents the Greek "the good thing," that is, the favor, the kindness, that Paul is requesting of Philemon.

Of your own free will represents the opposite of "compulsion." Only here in the NT does the phrase occur; see the adverb hekousiōs in Heb

10.26; 1 Peter 5.2. Of your own free will may be rendered as "because you want to do so" or "because that is what you would like to do."

You agree (TEV) or "your consent" (RSV) represents the Greek tēs sēs gnomēs. The noun means "idea, opinion," and here it clearly means agreement, consent, permission. Paul will not act without Philemon's approval. The double negative in the final sentence of verse 14 involving not. unless may be restructured as an affirmative, for example, "so I will only do what you agree I should do."

1.15   It may be that Onesimus was away from you for
             a short time so that you might have him back for
             all time.

"Perhaps" (RSV) represents Greek tacha (here and in Rom 5.7). The potentiality suggested by the introductory expression it may be that is often better expressed by an adverb such as "perhaps."

Was away (from you)...you might have him back refer to two contrasting situations: the first during the time Onesimus was in flight from Philemon and the second when he is to return to his master. It seems quite clear that the way in which Paul phrases the matter [particularly in the use of the cautious "perhaps," the use of the passive form of the verb "to be separated," and the avoidance of the verb "he ran away (from you)"] implies that in all this God was at work to bring about the intended result which Paul so ardently hopes to achieve.

Was away from you may be expressed more effectively as a negation, for example, "was not with you" or "did not remain there with you."

Onesimus' separation was for a short time (literally "for an hour," see also 2 Cor 7.8); his return will hold good for all time (RSV "for ever"). It is difficult to determine exactly what Paul meant by this "eternally"; perhaps something like "for good," "permanently" (see a similar use in John 8.35). In any case the new relationship, that of Christian brothers, is a permanent one, which will not change regardless of whatever else may change.

For a short time must not be understood as merely a brief period of a day or so. Obviously Onesimus had traveled some distance from Colossae and had probably been with Paul for some time. If a somewhat definite expression of time must be employed, it should reflect at least several weeks and possibly several months.

For all time may be expressed as "from now on" or "continuously."

You might have him back may be expressed in many languages as "he might be again with you" or "he might remain with you."

1.16   And now he is not just a slave, but much more than
             a slave: he is a dear brother in Christ. How much
             he means to me! And how much more he will mean to
             you, both as a slave and as a brother in the Lord!

This verse continues from verse 15 as the completion of the sentence, "so that you might have him back for ever, (16) no longer as a slave but..." (as RSV has done). It should be noticed that if the RSV

translation is taken literally, it means that Paul is telling Philemon
that Onesimus is to be in deed and in fact a free man. But this does
not seem to be what Paul means, and Lohse quotes with approval the com-
ment of H. von Soden that the particle as "expresses the subjective
evaluation of the relationship without calling its objective form
into question...and therefore the line of thought found in 1 Cor 7.20-
24 is not exceeded"[15] (see also Lightfoot, Vincent). TEV has tried to indicate this by and now he is not just a slave (compare Phps "not merely
as a slave"; GeCL "So now he is for you much more than a slave, that is,
a beloved brother").

The negative-positive contrast in the TEV and now he is not just a
slave, but much more than a slave may require an inversion in some lan-
gauges, for example, "and now he is much more than a slave, he is not
just a slave" or "...not a slave only." By placing the positive statement before the negative, the meaning of the entire expression may often
be more readily understood.

In some languages a slave is described as "one who must work without pay," but more often a term for slave refers to "an owned person" or
"a person who belongs to someone else." The first part of verse 16 may,
therefore, be rendered as "and now he is much more than just a person
whom you own."

A dear brother in Christ: Onesimus is now Philemon's Christian
brother, and it is this fact which must determine their relationship
from now on. A dear brother in Christ may be equivalent to " a dear
fellow believer in Christ," or "a fellow believer in Christ who is dear
to you," or "a Christian fellow believer dear to you."

The second part of the verse could be translated, "he means so
much to me, but he will mean much more to you..."; compare NIV "He is
very dear to me but even dearer to you..." In a number of languages, it
is far more meaningful to use an intensive expression together with a
comparative rather than to employ an exclamation, for example, "he means
very much to me, and he will mean even more to you." To express the concept involved in the verb mean, it may be useful to speak of "value,"
for example, "he is so valuable to me, but he will be even more valuable
to you."

Both as a slave and as a brother in the Lord translates what is
literally "both in the flesh and in the Lord" (so RSV). The Greek "in
the flesh" means Onesimus' natural status as a slave; he is still a
slave (compare Lohse), but now he is also a dear Christian brother, which
is something altogether new for Philemon. The translation should reflect
the fact that nowhere in this letter does Paul tell Philemon, in so many
words, to set Onesimus free, nor does he take it for granted that Philemon will do so. Rather he seems to take it for granted that Onesimus will
continue to be Philemon's slave, even though their relationship is now
transformed by the fact that Onesimus is a Christian. (In verse 21, however, Paul may be hinting that he hopes that Philemon will set Onesimus
free.) Lightfoot quotes Meyer on this double relationship "in the flesh
and in the Lord": "In the former...Philemon had the brother for a slave;
in the latter, he had the slave for a brother."[16] Their relation as Christian brothers transcended and transformed but did not replace their relationship as master and slave.

Both as a slave and as a brother in the Lord may be rendered as "he is your slave and he is also your fellow believer in the Lord." This expression both as a slave and as a brother in the Lord should be combined with the concept of the value which Onesimus will now constitute for Philemon. The meaning may be expressed in some instances as "very much appreciated both as your slave as well as your fellow believer in the Lord."

"Your fellow believer in the Lord" may also be rendered as "one who believes in the Lord even as you do."

1.17   So, if you think of me as your partner, welcome
             him back just as you would welcome me.

On the basis of his relationship with Philemon as a partner, Paul appeals to him to give Onesimus the same kind of welcome he would give Paul, that is, receive him as a brother and a partner. The word partner translates the Greek koinōnos, cognate of the noun koinōnia "sharing, fellowship" in verse 6 (compare 2 Cor 8.23 where Paul calls Titus his partner; in Luke 5.10 James and John are called Simon Peter's partners). Paul is talking about partnership in the Christian faith and work. Paul phrases the matter as if it were in doubt, but this is a rhetorical device (compare a similar kind of statement in Col 2.20).

A literal rendering of the conditional clause if you think of me as your partner might suggest that this would not be the case. In order to indicate clearly the implication of what Paul is saying, one may translate "you think of me as your partner and therefore..." The expression partner often requires some kind of descriptive equivalent, for example, "as one who works together with you for the Lord."

Welcome him back may be rendered in some instances as "receive him gladly" or, as in some languages, "when he returns, say to him,'You are in your own home'" or "...my home is your home." These types of formulaic statements are frequently the way in which people welcome a guest.

1.18   If he has done you any wrong or owes you anything,
             charge it to my account.

Paul deals with a delicate subject by treating it as doubtful, which it most certainly was not, for it was the common thing for a runaway slave to take with him some valuables or money from his master.

Done you any wrong translates the verb adikeō (see Col 3.25), a general term covering every possible misdeed. Owes you anything refers specifically to theft; Paul avoids calling it robbery.

Charge it to my account is used figuratively; it is a term borrowed from the business world and simply means that Paul will assume the responsibility for making good any loss suffered by Philemon as a result of Onesimus' action.

If the conditional clause if he has done you any wrong or owes you anything might suggest that he did not do any wrong, it is better to use some kind of indefinite clause, for example, "whatever wrong he has done you or whatever he owes you."

Charge it to my account is often expressed somewhat idiomatically, for example, "put my name beside the sum" or "tell me how much I owe you."

1.19   Here, I will write this with my own hand: <u>I, Paul,</u>
<u>will pay you back</u>. (I should not have to remind
you, of course, that you owe your very self to me.)

Here Paul takes the stylus and writes these words himself (see Col
4.18). The aorist tense of the verb "to write" is another instance of
the epistolary aorist (see verse 12). Only here in the NT does the verb
<u>apotinō</u> "to repay" occur.

<u>I will write this with my own hand</u> may be expressed as "I myself
am writing the following words." In some languages, <u>with my own hand</u> is
expressed "with my own fingers" or even "with my own arm." It is important to use the expression which is most in keeping with receptor-lan-
guage usage.

<u>I, Paul, will pay you back</u> may be rendered as "I, Paul, will pay
you." A literal rendering of "pay back" might suggest that this was a
debt which Paul himself had incurred and not on behalf of Onesimus. It
may be necessary to refer to what is to be paid as, "I will pay you
whatever is owed" or "I will pay you all that money."

Then Paul adds, almost as an afterthought, a reminder to Philemon:
"I am now indebted to you; but don't forget that your debt to me is much
greater--you owe me you very self." Paul is referring to the fact that
he had been instrumental in Philemon's conversion, so that Philemon owes
his spiritual life to Paul.

The phrase translated <u>I should not have to remind you</u> is used also
in 2 Cor 9.4. It may be expressed as "surely it is not necessary for me
to mention to you" or "...to tell you."

The verb <u>owe</u> in this verse translates the compound <u>prosopheilō</u>
which occurs only here in the NT; the simple <u>opheilō</u> is used in verse 18.
It may be rather difficult to speak of "owing oneself." The TEV rendering
<u>that you owe your very self to me</u> may, however, be restructured as "you
are in debt to me for your life." But a literal rendering of "for your
life" might suggest that Paul himself had at one time rescued Philemon
from death. It may, therefore, be essential to indicate precisely what is
involved, for example, "you are in debt to me for your new life through
Christ" or "...for your life as a Christian."

1.20   So, my brother, please do me this favor for the
Lord's sake; as a brother in Christ, cheer me up!

<u>Do me this favor</u> translates the passive of the verb <u>oninēmi</u>, used
only here in the NT (see verse 11), "may I be benefited, profited" (by
you). <u>Please do me this favor</u> may be expressed as "be so good as to help
me in this way" or "I ask you to help me in this way."

<u>For the Lord's sake</u> is literally in Greek "in the Lord" (see RSV).
It may be translated "as a fellow Christian" (see TNT). Or it may be
rendered as "as a way of serving the Lord."

Instead of "in Christ" (RSV), later manuscripts have "in the Lord"
(see KJV). <u>As a brother in Christ</u> may be rendered as "as a fellow believer."

Cheer me up is the same expression as in verse 7, "refresh my heart." It may be expressed simply as "make me happy," but frequently the equivalent of cheer me up is an idiomatic expression, "cause my heart to sing" or "give my heart sweetness."

1.21   I am sure, as I write this, that you will do
            what I ask--in fact I know that you will do even
            more.

Some commentators (for example, Vincent, Moule, Lohse; see NAB) take verse 21 to be the beginning of a new section, but it seems preferable to keep it (together with the closely related verse 22) as the conclusion of the main section, since there is no abrupt shift in subject matter.
As I write this should not be translated in such a way as to indicate that Paul was himself writing out the letter. It was obviously dictated since in verse 19 Paul specifically refers to something which he himself wrote as a part of the letter. Accordingly, one may translate as I write this as "as I send this letter to you."
You will do what I ask translates "your obedience" (RSV). Paul takes it for granted that Philemon will comply with his request to receive Onesimus back as he would receive Paul (verse 17).
But, Paul adds, I know that you will do even more. It would seem that Paul is thinking of the possibility that Philemon will set Onesimus free so that Onesimus can return to Paul and help him (verse 13). It may be necessary in some languages to indicate what is specifically involved in the comparison, for example, "I know that you will do even more than what I have asked you to do" or, as expressed in some languages, "I know that in what you will do you will surpass even what I have asked of you."

1.22   At the same time, get a room ready for me, be-
            cause I hope that God will answer the prayers
            of all of you and give me back to you.

Some translations (JB TOB) take verse 22 as the beginning of a new section; but it is so closely related to verse 21 that it should not be separated from it.
At the same time, that is, while making the former request, he adds this other request. The meaning is better represented by such translations as NEB NIV "one thing more"; JB "there is another thing"; Phps "will you do something else?" At the same time, get a room ready for me may be rendered as "I also want you to prepare a room for me" or "...get a guest room ready for me."
The request is get a room ready for me; Paul hopes soon to be a guest in Philemon's home, as a result of God's answer to the prayers of all of you. Here Paul uses the plural second person pronoun, whereas up till now, from verse 2, he has used the singular pronoun, referring only to Philemon. All of you would include Philemon, Apphia, Archippus, and the other members of the church.
In a number of languages, it is extremely difficult to find an

[131]

1.22

adequate term for hope. The closest equivalent may be a phrase such as
"I wait with confidence," for hope in its NT meaning implies a confident
expectation with regard to some future benefit. A verb such as "wait"
indicates future expectation, and "confidence" suggests that in the end
there will be some positive benefit.

In translating God will answer the prayers of all of you it is important to employ a word for answer which suggests more than merely re-
sponding to a question. Therefore, God will answer the prayers of all of
you may be translated as "God will do for you all that you pray to him
about."

I hope that God...will give me back to you translates the Greek
passive "I hope...to be given to you." The verb used, charizomai, means
"to make a gift, grant a favor" (in Col 2.13, 3.13 it is used in the
sense it often has of "to forgive"). It is a kindness, a favor, that the
people are asking God to grant them, namely, that Paul will be given his
freedom and be able to come to them. The you is again plural.

A literal rendering of I hope that God will answer the prayers of
all of you and give me back to you might suggest that Paul is hoping for
two different things, namely, that God will answer the prayers of the
believers and that he will give Paul back to the believers. Obviously,
of course, what the people are praying for is that he will be given back
to them. This relationship can perhaps be best expressed in some languages
as "that God will do what you have asked him to do, namely, to give me
back to you." On the other hand, a literal rendering of give me back to
you might seem very strange, for this is essentially a causative expression involving a return. Therefore, one may best translate give me
back to you as "cause me to return to you" or "allow me to return to you."

TEV	(1.23-25)	RSV

FINAL GREETINGS

23 Epaphras, who is in prison with me for the sake of Christ Jesus, sends you his greetings, 24 and so do my fellow workers Mark, Aristarchus, Demas, and Luke.
25 May the grace of the Lord Jesus Christ be with you all.

23 Epaphras, my fellow prisoner in Christ Jesus, sends greetings to you, 24 and so do Mark, Aristarchus, Demas, and Luke, my fellow workers.
25 The grace of the Lord Jesus Christ be with your spirit.

The concluding section of the letter transmits the greetings sent
from people who are with Paul (verses 23-24), and ends with a benediction
(verse 25).

1.23-24   Epaphras, who is in prison with me for the
sake of Christ Jesus, sends you his greetings,
24 and so do my fellow workers Mark, Aristarchus,
Demas and Luke.

The five men here named are also named in Colossians: Epaphras
(Col 1.7-8, 4.12-13), Mark and Aristarchus (Col 4.10), and Demas and
Luke (Col 4.14). It is strange that Jesus/Justus (Col 4.11) is omitted
here, and it has been conjectured that the Greek text en Christō Iēsou,
Markos "in Christ Jesus, (and) Mark" was originally (or was originally
meant to be) en Christō, Iēsous, Markos "in Christ, (and) Jesus, Mark."
No translation, however, has adopted this conjecture, not even as a
possible variant reading in the margin.

Epaphras is a "fellow prisoner" (RSV) of Paul's (as Aristarchus is
called in Col 4.10) for the sake of Christ Jesus, that is, because of
his Christian work. Who is in prison with me may be expressed as "who is
in prison here where I am in prison," and for the sake of Christ Jesus
may be rendered as "because he has told the good news about Christ Jesus"
or "because he has preached about Christ Jesus."

Sends you: the you is here singular, meaning Philemon. Sends you
his greetings may be expressed in a number of ways: "says he wants you
to know that he thinks of you," or "wants to tell you he wishes you
well," or "wants you to know that he wants the best for you."

For fellow workers see verse 1 (and Col 4.11). And so do my fellow
workers Mark, Aristarchus, Demas, and Luke may be expressed as "those
who work with me, namely, Mark, Aristarchus, Demas, and Luke also want
me to tell you that they wish you well."

1.25   May the grace of the Lord Jesus Christ be
            with you all.

For the concluding benediction see Col 4.18. Here, as in other
letters, Paul prays that the grace of the Lord Jesus Christ be with them.
(Some later manuscripts have "our Lord Jesus Christ," see KJV.) The
benediction May the grace of the Lord Jesus Christ be with you all must
be introduced in a number of languages by some verb of prayer or petition,
for example, "I pray that the grace of the Lord Jesus Christ may be with
you all." Grace must often be expressed as an action or an event, and
therefore the structure of this benediction must be considerably changed,
for example, "I pray that the Lord Jesus Christ may show his grace to you
all" or "...show kindness to you all."

TEV has you all (also TNT) to show that the pronoun in Greek is
plural. The language of the Greek "with your spirit" (RSV) is used only
in Gal 6.18; Phil 4.23. In English, at least, "with your spirit" carries
overtones and implications not present in Paul's use of the words (see
Lohse); the Greek expression means simply "with you" (plural).

NOTES

1. B. M. Newman, The Bible Translator, 25(2).240-245.

2. B. M. Newman, personal correspondence.

3. J. B. Lightfoot, Commentary on Colossians and Philemon, p. 133.

4. T. K. Abbott, Commentary on Ephesians and Colossians, p. 236.

5. C. F. D. Moule, Commentary on Colossians and Philemon, p. 99.

6. Moule, op. cit., p. 108.

7. Moule, op. cit., p. 114.

8. Lightfoot, op. cit., p. 209.

9. Quoted by Abbott, op. cit., p. 144.

10. Moule, op. cit., p. 121.

11. Lightfoot, op. cit., p. 221.

12. Lightfoot, op. cit., p. 280.

13. Moule, op. cit., p. 142.

14. John Knox, Commentary on Philemon, p. 566.

15. Eduard Lohse, Commentary on Colossians and Philemon, p. 203.

16. Lightfoot, op. cit., p. 341.

BIBLIOGRAPHY

BIBLE TEXTS AND VERSIONS CITED

(Unless otherwise indicated in the text, references are to the most recent edition listed. CL = Common Language Translation.)

Text

The Greek New Testament. 1st edition 1966; 3rd edition 1975. K. Aland, M. Black, C. M. Martini, B. M. Metzger, and A. Wikgren, eds. Stuttgart: United Bible Societies.

Versions

La Bible de Jérusalem. 1973. Paris: Les Editions du Cerf. Cited as BJ.

A Biblia Na Linguagem De Hoje. O Novo Testamento. 1973. Rio de Janeiro: Sociedade Bíblica do Brasil. Cited as BrCL.

Bonnes Nouvelles Aujourd'hui. Le Nouveau Testament traduit en français courant d'après le texte grec. 1971. Paris, etc.: Les Sociétés Bibliques. Cited as FrCL.

Dios Llega Al Hombre. El Nuevo Testamento de Nuestro Señor Jesucristo: Versión Popular. 1st edition 1966; 2nd edition 1970. Asunción, etc.: Sociedades Bíblicas Unidas. European edition 1971. Madrid: Sociedad Bíblica. Cited as SpCL.

Good News for Modern Man: The New Testament in Today's English Version. 1st edition 1966; 3rd edition 1971. New York: American Bible Society. 1st British edition 1968; 3rd British edition 1972. London: Collins. Cited as TEV.

Groot Nieuws voor U. Het nieuwe testament in de omgangstaal. 1972. Amsterdam/Boxtel: Katholieke Bijbelstichting and Nederlansche Bijbelgenootschap. Cited as DuCL.

Die Gute Nachricht: Das Neue Testament in heutigem Deutsch. 1971. Stuttgart: Bibelanstalt. Cited as GeCL.

The Jerusalem Bible. 1966. London: Darton, Longman & Todd. Cited as JB.

King James Version. 1611. Cited as KJV.

LXX: Septuagint (editio quarta). 1950. Alfred Rahlfs, edidit. Stuttgart: Württembergische Bibelanstalt.

[137]

The New American Bible. 1970. Paterson, New Jersey: St. Anthony Guild Press. Cited as NAB.

The New English Bible. 1st edition of New Testament 1961; 2nd edition 1970. London: Oxford University Press, and Cambridge University Press. Cited as NEB.

The New Testament: a new translation by William Barclay. Volume II: The Letters and the Revelation. 1969. London: Collins. Cited as Brc.

The New Testament: a new translation by James Moffatt. 1922. London: Hodder & Stoughton. New edition, revised: 1934. New York: Harper and Row. Cited as Mft.

New Testament: An American Translation. 1923. Edgar J. Goodspeed. Chicago: University Press. Cited as Gdp.

New Testament in Modern English. 1962. J. B. Phillips. New York: The Macmillan Co. Cited as Phps.

New Testament in Modern Speech. R. F. Weymouth. 1929. Newly revised by J. A. Roberston, 5th edition. London. Cited as Wey.

New International Version. 1973. Grand Rapids, Michigan: Zondervan Bible Publishers. Cited as NIV.

Revised Standard Version. 1952. New York: Nelson & Sons. Cited as RSV.

Twentieth Century New Testament. 1904. Chicago: Moody Press. Cited as TC.

Traduction Oecuménique de la Bible: Nouveau Testament. Paris: Sociétés Bibliques/Les Editions du Cerf. Cited as TOB.

The Translator's New Testament. 1973. London: British & Foreign Bible Society. Cited as TNT.

Vulgate: Novum Testamentum Latine, secundum editionem Sancti Hieronymi (editio minor). 1950. J. Wordsworth and J. J. White, eds. Oxford. Cited as Vg.

GENERAL BIBLIOGRAPHY

Grammars

Blass, F. and A. Debrunner. 1961. A Greek Grammar of the New Testament and other Early Christian Literature. Chicago: University of Chicago Press. (English translation by Robert W. Funk.)

Moule, C. F. D. 1953. An Idiom-Book of New Testament Greek. Cambridge, England: Cambridge University Press.

Moulton, J. H. 1st edition 1906; 3rd edition 1908. A Grammar of New Testament Greek, Vol. 1. J. H. Moulton and W. F. Howard. 1st edition 1920, 2nd edition 1920, Vol. 2. N. Turner. 1963, Vol. 3. Edinburgh: T. & T. Clark.

Commentaries

Abbott, T. K. 1916. Ephesians and Colossians (International Critical Commentary). New York: Charles Scribner's Sons.

Beare, F. W. 1955. Colossians (Interpreter's Bible, vol. XI). New York: Abingdon Cokesbury.

Knox, John. 1955. Philemon (Interpreter's Bible, vol. XI). New York: Abingdon Cokesbury.

Lightfoot, J. B. 1892. Colossians and Philemon. London: Macmillan & Co.

Lohse, Eduard. 1971. Colossians and Philemon (Hermeneia). Philadelphia: Fortress Press. (English translation by Wm. T. Poehlmann and Robert J. Karris.)

Metzger, B. M. 1971. A Textual Commentary on the Greek New Testament. London and New York: United Bible Societies.

Moule, C. F. D. 1957. Colossians and Philemon (Cambridge Greek Testament). Cambridge: University Press.

Vincent, Marvin R. 1897. Philemon (International Critical Commentary). Edinburgh: T. & T. Clark.

GLOSSARY

accusative form is the form a word takes in biblical Greek (as well as
other languages) when the word functions as the direct object of a
verb. For example, in English "John gave the boy a ball," "a ball"
is the direct object of the verb "gave"; if this sentence were written
in Greek the word "a ball" would be written out in the accusative
form.

active voice see voice.

adjective is a word which limits, describes, or qualifies a noun. In
English, "red," "tall," "beautiful," "important," etc. are adjectives.

adverb is a word which limits, describes, or modifies a verb, an adjective,
or another adverb. In English, "quickly," "soon," "primarily," "very,"
etc. are adverbs.

adverbial refers to adverbs. An adverbial phrase is a phrase which
functions as an adverb.

anomalous is an adjective meaning irregular, abnormal, extraordinary, not
conforming to the usual rule. It would be anomalous for a mule to run
in a horse race.

aorist refers to a set of forms in Greek verbs which denote an action
completed without the implication of continuance or duration. Usually,
but not always, the action is considered as completed in past time.

apposition is the placing of two expressions together so that they both
identify the same object or event, for example, "my friend, Mr. Smith."
The one expression is said to be the appositive of the other.

attribution, attributive. An attributive is a term which limits or describes another term. In "the big man ran slowly," the adjective "big"
is an attributive of "man" and the adverb "slowly" is an attributive
of "ran." Attribution, therefore, is the act of assigning a certain
quality or character to an object or an event.

causative relates to events and indicates that someone caused something
to happen, rather than that he did it himself. In "John ran the horse,"
the verb "ran" is a causative, since it was not John who ran, but
rather it was John who caused the horse to run.

chiastic construction is a reversal of the order of words or phrases in
an otherwise parallel construction. Example: "I (1) / was shapen (2)
/ in iniquity (3) // in sin (3)/ did my mother conceive (2) / me (1)."

circumcise. To cut off the foreskin of a Jewish baby boy as a sign of
God's covenant with the people of Israel.

circumstantial is an adjective which refers to any kind of circumstance which modifies an event. In grammatical terms, for example, "When the sun rose, the boy woke up" the temporal clause "When the sun rose" is a circumstantial clause, modifying the main action "the boy woke up."

clause is a grammatical construction normally consisting of a subject and a predicate. An independent clause may stand alone as a sentence, but a dependent clause (functioning as a noun, adjective, or adverb) does not form a complete sentence.

cognate languages are those which are closely related and have many features of grammar and vocabulary which are similar. French and Spanish are cognate languages, as also are English and German.

concessive means expressing a concession, that is, the allowance or admission of something which is a variance with the principal thing stated. Concession is usually expressed in English by "though" ("even though," "although"). Example: "Though the current was swift, James was able to cross the stream."

conditional refers to a clause or phrase which expresses or implies a condition, in English usually introduced by "if."

context is that which precedes and/or follows any part of a discourse. For example, the context of a word or phrase in Scripture would be the other words and phrases associated with it in the sentence, paragraph, section, and even the entire book in which it occurs. The context of a term often affects its meaning, so that it does not mean exactly the same thing in one context as it does in another.

contrastive expresses something opposed to or in contrast to something already stated. "But" and "however" are contrastive conjunctions.

copyists were men who made handwritten copies of books, before the invention of printing. They were also called "scribes." See manuscript.

cultic is an adjective formed from the noun "cult"; it is used to describe any custom or action which is required in the performance of religious practices. It is broadly synonymous with the adjectives "ritual" and "ceremonial."

dative case is the form a word takes in biblical Greek (as well as other languages) when the word functions as the indirect object of a verb. For example, in English "John gave the boy a ball," "the boy" is the indirect object of the verb "gave" ("a ball" being the direct object); if this sentence were written in Greek the words "the boy" would be written out in the dative form.

designation means properly the act of designating, that is, of marking out, defining, specifying.

[142]

discourse is the connected and continuous communication of thought by
means of language, whether spoken or written. The way in which the
elements of a discourse are arranged is called discourse structure.
Direct discourse is the reproduction of the actual words of one person
embedded in the discourse of another person. For example, "He declared,
'I will have nothing to do with this man.'" Indirect discourse is the
reporting of the words of one person embedded in the discourse of another person in an altered grammatical form. For example, "He said
he would have nothing to do with that man."

ellipsis (plural ellipses) or elliptical expression refers to words or
phrases normally omitted in a discourse when the sense is perfectly
clear without them. In the following sentence, the words within
brackets are elliptical: "If (it is) necessary (for me to do so), I
will wait up all night." What is elliptical in one language may need
to be expressed in another.

epistolary "we" is the use of the pronoun "we" ("us," "our") instead of
"I" ("me," "my") in writing by a single person, for the purpose of
achieving a more formal or impersonal effect. Also called "editorial
'we'."

exclusive first person plural excludes the person(s) addressed. That is,
a speaker may use "we" to refer to himself and his companions, while
specifically excluding the person(s) to whom he is speaking. See inclusive first person plural.

exegesis, exegete, exegetical. The process of determining the meaning
of a text (or the result of this process), normally in terms of "who
said what to whom under what circumstances and with what intent," is
called exegesis. A correct exegesis is indispensable before a passage
can be translated correctly. Exegetes are people who devote their
labors to exegesis. Exegetical refers to exegesis.

exhortation is the verbal act of encouraging, attempting, urging, to
make someone change a course of action or a matter of belief.

exposition is the act of systematically setting forth an idea or concept;
it means to explain, define, clarify.

first person. See person.

idiom or idiomatic expression is a combination of terms whose meanings
cannot be derived by adding up the meanings of the parts. "To hang
one's head," "to have a green thumb," and "behind the eight ball" are
English idioms. Idioms almost always lose their meaning completely
when translated literally from one language to another.

imperative refers to forms of a verb which indicate commands or requests.
In "go and do likewise," the verbs "go" and "do" are imperatives. In
most languages imperatives are confined to the grammatical second person;
but some languages have corresponding forms for the first and third persons.

inclusive first person plural includes both the speaker and the one(s) to whom he is speaking. See exclusive first person plural.

indirect discourse. See discourse.

injunction may refer in a general way to the act of urging or encouraging someone to do something, or to the more restricted sense of an authoritative order or command which must be obeyed.

intensive compound refers to the form of a word in which two elements are combined, one of which has the effect of making stronger the action expressed by the simple form of the word. For example, "hyperactive" is an intensive compound meaning "very active."

interpretation of a text is the exegesis of it. See exegesis.

intransitive refers to a verb which does not have or need a direct object to complete its meaning, for example, "he lives." See transitive.

inversion in discourse is to restructure one form into its opposite; for example, to change a passive into an active (as "he was struck by a ball" to "a ball struck him").

literal means the ordinary or primary meaning of a term or expression, in contrast to a figurative meaning. In translation, literal is following the exact words and word order of the source language.

manuscript is a book, document, letter, etc. written by hand. Thousands of manuscript copies of various New Testament books are still in existence, but none of the original manuscripts. See copyists.

middle voice. See voice.

noun is a word that is the name of a subject of discourse, as a person, place, thing, idea, etc.

participial phrase is a phrase governed by a participle. See participle.

participle is a verbal adjective, that is, a word which retains some of the characteristics of a verb while functioning as an adjective. In "singing waters" and "painted desert," "singing" and "painted" are participles.

passive voice. See voice.

perfective participle is a participle in the perfect tense. See participle and perfect tense.

perfect tense is a set of verb forms which indicate an action already completed when another occurs. The perfect tense in Greek also indicates that the action continues into the present.

[144]

person, a grammatical term, refers to the speaker, the person spoken to, or the person(s) or thing(s) spoken about. First person is the person(s) or thing(s) speaking ("I," "me," "my," "mine"; "we," "us," "our," "ours"). Second person is the person(s) or thing(s) spoken to ("thou," "thee," "thy," "thine"; "ye," "you," "your," "yours"). Third person is the person(s) or thing(s) spoken about ("he," "she," "it," "his," "her," "them," "their," etc.). The examples here given are all pronouns, but in many languages the verb forms distinguish between the persons and also indicate whether they are singular or plural.

plural refers to the form of a word which indicates more than one, in contrast to singular, which indicates just one.

pronouns are words which are used in place of nouns, such as "he," "him," "his," "she," "we," "them," "who," "which," "this," "these," etc.

qualitative and quantitative are terms which are frequently used in contrast to each other. Qualitative has to do with quality, and quantitative with quantity. Certain words ("great," for example) are sometimes used qualitatively ("a great man") and at other times quantitatively ("a great pile").

receptor is the person(s) receiving a message. The receptor language is the language into which a translation is made. The receptor culture is the culture of the people for whom a translation is made, especially when it differs radically from the culture of the people for whom the original message was written.

running head is a phrase or sentence that may be placed at the top of a page to indicate in a general way the contents of the page over which it appears. Both the RSV and the NEB use running-heads.

Septuagint is a translation of the Old Testament into Greek, made some two hundred years before Christ. It is often abbreviated as LXX.

simile (pronounced SIM-i-lee) is a figure of speech which describes one event or object by comparing it to another, as "she runs like a deer," "he is as straight as an arrow." Similes are less subtle than metaphors in that they use "like," "as," or some other word to mark or signal the comparison.

stereotype is a metal printing plate; the word is used in a figurative way meaning a standard or conventional way of stating a matter, usually in a very simple way that fails adequately to explain the matter.

subordinate structure designates a clause connected with and dependent on another clause.

substantive is a noun or anything (pronoun, phrase, clause, adjective, etc.) that functions as a noun.

supplication is the act of asking, begging, requesting; it is often used to refer to prayer.

temporal refers to time. Temporal relations are the relations of time between events. A temporal clause is a dependent clause which indicates the time of the action in the main clause.

tense is usually a form of a verb which indicates time relative to a discourse or some event in a discourse. The most common forms of tense are past, present, and future.

transformation is a process of grammatical modification, usually beginning with the so-called deep structures and proceeding to the more elaborate surface structure. For example, a basic expression such as John hit Bill could be transformed into Wasn't Bill hit by John? This would involve three primary transformations: (1) active to passive, (2) positive to negative, and (3) statement to question. A back-transformation is the reverse of this process.

transition in discourse is passing from one thought or group of related thoughts to another. In written discourse, the use of marks of punctuation and the division into paragraphs help to mark the transitions. Transitional particles such as prepositions and conjunctions ("in," "by," "so," "because," "furthermore," "however," etc.) and transitional phrases ("in other words," "in the meantime," "at last," etc.) serve a like purpose.

transitive refers to a verb which requires a direct object to complete its meaning. "Hit," for example, is transitive. If one says, "he hits," the question arises, "he hits what?" Many verbs may be either transitive or intransitive, depending on how they are used. For example, "she sings folk songs" (transitive) and "she sings beautifully" (intransitive). See intransitive.

transliteration is to represent a word from the source language in the letters of the receptor language rather than to translate its meaning.

verbs are a grammatical class of words which express existence, action, or occurrence, as "be," "become," "run," "think," etc.

vocative refers to the person addressed (spoken to). Some languages have distinctive vocative forms for nouns.

voice in grammar is the relation of the action expressed by a verb to the participants in the action. In English and many other languages, the active voice indicates that the subject performs the action ("John hit the man"), while the passive voice indicates that the subject is being acted upon ("the man was hit"). The Greek language has a middle voice, in which the subject may be regarded as doing something to or for himself (or itself).

INDEX